FOR GOD'S SAKE, ASK!

FOR GOD'S SAKE, ASK!

Alastair Symington

in conversation with
Rikki Fulton

SAINT ANDREW PRESS
EDINBURGH

First published in 1993 by
SAINT ANDREW PRESS
121 George Street, Edinburgh EH2 4YN

Copyright © Alastair Symington 1993

ISBN 0 7152 0686 9

British Library Catalogue in Publication Data
A catalogue record
for this book is available
from the British Library.

ISBN 0715206869

Bible references used throughout this book have been taken from the **Revised Standard Version (RSV)**, copyright 1946, 1952, © 1971, by the Division of Christian Education of the National Council of the Churches of Christ in the USA, and are used by permission.

Cover design by Mark Blackadder.
Cover photographs by Simon Jones.
This book has been set in 11.5/14 pt Garamond.
Printed and Bound in Great Britain by
Athenaeum Press Ltd, Newcastle upon Tyne.

Contents

Foreword

When I was a child, I spake as a child, I understood as a child, I thought as a child: but when I became a man, I put away childish things.

~ 1 Corinthians ~

I CONFESS I mourned as, one by one, the magical creatures of childhood were made compulsorily redundant, and the wishing rights in secret places withdrawn along with the personal PO Box to Father Christmas. In those days unicorns and fairies and elves were happily grouped together with Angels and Jesus and God, providing courts of appeal of ever higher authority for frustrated, despairing children. Faith presents few problems in childhood; the problem comes later when the child is taught that all the delightful, dependable, magical characters were, alas, imaginary—with One Exception. And that the most unbelievable of all!

As the years passed and I busily sought a place in the world, the last and most sublime of these concepts was smothered by more immediate essentials. But they left behind a strange after-taste of wistful longing which was sufficient to galvanise me into action at the very sight of a dog-collar. I would confront the hapless minister and demand to know why *I* should believe in God, and what evidence could he offer in support of his answer. Not surprisingly, in every case it appeared I had made my approach on the very day the unfortunate gentleman was already late for an important luncheon or meeting of the General Assembly.

Happily, later encounters proved more fulfilling.

A jovial Irish priest, in answer to the question 'Why should I believe in God', answered bluntly, 'Why not?' And an evangelist of quite striking personality blinded me with so much theological science, I wondered if reading Tolkien might not be simpler —although I am happy to say that we became good friends.

And then (make of this what you will) I happened to join Jimmy Mack, the popular broadcaster, in the BBC canteen one day. Our meeting was fortuitous, he said, and proceeded to ask me to open his church's Summer fête, a chore I would gladly have undertaken but could not. His church, it transpired, was New Kilpatrick in Bearsden, Glasgow, and Jimmy was (and is) an elder there.

I asked if Kate, my wife, and I might visit and we were very warmly welcomed. That was the first time I heard the Revd Alastair Symington preach.

If you understand the phrase 'coming home'—and I am sure you do—you will understand our feelings about this church and its minister. The warmth and friendliness of that vast congregation filled with children, young people and adults, was indeed like a homecoming.

And from that day Sunday has become, for us, the most important, indeed the most completely fulfilling and enjoyable day of the week.

Alastair Symington has long since become a great and close friend. A man of courage, he is never one to duck an argument and our debates are lively, exciting and informative.

His message is one of simplicity and tremendous optimism— a much needed bulwark against the Calvinist concoction of fire and brimstone. I have seen our congregation—ourselves included—leave the church walking some two feet above the hallowed ground after a service conducted by this man. He is a young man compared with me, but older by far in his great wisdom. A brilliant scholar, a stimulating debater, a powerful writer and preacher, and a delightful humourist ...

... if only I could think of something nice to say about him. Well, what do you know—here come the unicorns!

Rikki Fulton OBE
Glasgow 1993

Introduction

RIKKI Fulton is the only person I have ever met who has a consistently inquisitive longing to know a bit more about the Amalekites. For those of us who have heard the name of this tribe, but are not so sure where their story is to be found—or, indeed, what it's all about—then I can save you searching Scripture: the passage which gives rise to the questions is in 1 Samuel 15.

Rikki bombards me with question after question:

'What *about* the Amalekites? ... What sort of God could say that he wanted his servants to go and destroy a whole people? ... When Saul has spared the women and little children, how can God be so angry that he insists on them being slain? ... If the Bible is the Word of God, what do we make of Samuel hewing Agag in pieces before the Lord at Gilgal?'

Well, what can you do when faced with all this? First of all you can look at your watch and say to Rikki that you find the questions terribly interesting and most stimulating, but you have an urgent appointment that just cannot be broken. In his theatre days that's the tactic which he claims was used most readily and most often by ministers who claimed to be chaplains to these places. They promised to come back soon, perhaps even tomorrow, and Rikki is still waiting, he tells me. Try that tactic out and you can be sure that your credibility will be gone and one more church member will pass through your records, not to return.

The second thing you can do is panic and try to turn the question another way. Isn't that what every good politician, social worker, administrator or minister is taught to do? If you don't know the answer to the question, make up another question and answer it. This is what we have done in the Church, time after time, so that there are now thousands of unchurched souls in our society who are far from being spiritual morons, but who have found that their curiosity and their genuine soul-searching has been spurned. Either you don't know what to say to them, or you don't believe they should be asking these sorts of questions. Try that panic tactic out and you won't be let off the hook.

The third thing to do is to face up to the questions and knuckle down to the task in hand. It helps, of course, when Rikki offers you a fresh cup of coffee in the midst of it all, to marshal the thoughts and to keep up with his active mind.

There are always influences on us in our lives and, if you are a minister, these influences can be many and varied. So it must be when your involvement is so consistently with all sorts of people. Probably the most consistently honest influence that a minister has is from within his own family, and it is a wise man indeed who is prepare to listen to 'home' truths and be guided by them. But beyond the family, a minister may very occasionally be blessed with the sort of stimulus which comes from a man like Rikki Fulton. I count his friendship as something of inestimable value, not only for the warmth of his character, but also for the tremendous intellect and the very honest questions that pour from the man—the Amalekite issue included!

In the years I have known him he has worked a greater influence on my direction of thinking and preaching than any other person. To all of us who are his contemporaries, he is Scotland's greatest comedian, with gifts which seem limitless. To me, his minister, he is one of the few members of the Church I have met in the twenty years since my ordination who has dared to ask the deepest questions, who has articulated the most honest challenge and who has searched for the truth of God in such a positively provocative way that you find yourself doing the search all over again.

In conversation with him, I became more and more aware that the 'Revd I M Jolly', that well-known character created by Rikki, is a mirror for ministers to look at themselves deeper than perhaps they might like. Are we really like that—even if only a little? Is the laughter that 'Jolly' evokes in us all the heartier because people see in him what they sometimes see in us ministers? How often do we ministers make people feel hot with sin, rather than warm with a sense of the overwhelming love of God? Are we a morose bunch? Are we addressing any of the real questions that people have about the Christian faith, or do we simply teach and talk and preach according to what we imagine their questions are—or, even worse, what the questions *ought* to be? How interested are we in people who are searching for faith, or can we not honestly be bothered to take the time with them, because we cannot understand how they are so slow to see things as easily as we apparently do? And do we really see things that clearly anyway?

Again, Rikki Fulton raises enormously helpful images of how the public preaching of the Church is perceived. In his own written observations in Kenneth Roy's book *Conversations in a Small Country* (Carrick Publishing), Rikki Fulton uses a word which grips you, if you are sensitive to the great task which our Church has in today's society, when he observes that so frequently in his experience the Church has been 'downbeat' in its emphasis. I don't know for a fact if that is the case, because, as a minister, you do not have the opportunity as often as others to listen to a lot of what is preached in the name of the Church. But if even one of our members suggests it as a considered observation, then we ought to listen and, where necessary, take action. For the Church must be 'upbeat' in what it proclaims, otherwise its message is going to reach fewer and fewer, and its missionary task is going to be severely obstructed.

The following chapters comprise a compilation of some of the conversations which Rikki and I have enjoyed. His questions are short and very clear. The answers are a reflection on the sorts of thing I would be anxious to say to *any* person with genuine enquiries to make about the Christian faith. Some of what is written appeared in sermon form, directly in response to thoughts that had been formed in me because of Rikki's questions. Other parts are a summation of the things we said to each other in lengthy conversation. All of it tries to find its root in the Old and New Testaments, for it is there that both Rikki and I agree that we have to search for God's Word as it comes through all the fallibility and cultural restrictions of the various authors. Whether the chapters offer answers, or whether they simply extend the scope of the questioning, is for others to determine.

The chapters also follow a loose pattern of a year's conversations, and therefore cover not only general biblical questions and issues, but also the particular areas of the Christian Year. However they are arranged, the overriding compulsion to write down some answers arises from my own conviction that thousands of people are out there, looking for some sort of relationship with God. More than that, they need to feel that the Church is prepared to acknowledge the search and to go with people on their hunt after truth. It is one thing to dictate to people from the lofty heights of a pulpit but, just as Jesus Christ came as a listening and preaching Saviour to his people, the Church today needs to find itself far readier to listen to the longings of our people now.

It is a constantly thrilling thing to be adventurous in the search for truth and the Church might be a little surprised to know that there are many 'Rikki Fultons' knocking at our doors. He knocked at mine and I've enjoyed the encounter ever since.

Alastair Symington
Glasgow 1993

1

The New Year's Party
—then what?

R IKKI Fulton and his wife Kate came early on Hogmanay. It gave us time to sit and start the festivity, as millions in Scotland do, watching *Scotch and Wry* on television. Here was the man in full flight—a talented actor. Here was the array of his personality which captivated the hour so fully that by the time 'I M Jolly' presented his Last Call, you could scarcely believe the programme was over.

'What sort of day have you had ... ?' says Jolly morosely, before launching into another of his mirrors for ministers which the wiser among us look at lest we see anything of ourselves there, and the more foolish of the ministerial profession dismiss with a touch of haughtiness.

Then it is the New Year bells and a glass raised and before very long the conversation is underway again. Here's the start of a New Year with all the Scottish flair for optimism. The slate is wiped clean. The days and months stretch out in front of us and we can make a new start. But how can we be confident? How do we know? What makes us think that God is going to be able to influence the untouched weeks and months ahead? Is there real hope, or must we only look for chance and fate? Is there anything in the Bible ... ? And so the conversation goes along into the wee sma' hours. And it's great!

I always like to steer the questions to the Bible if we want to look for answers. It's not that we couldn't talk about a lot of other things from a lot of other perspectives, but the Bible is very much an unresearched source for the real enquirer. Even early on New Year's day, it's no bad place to start. And maybe because I have a special love for the Old Testament, or maybe it's because the Old Testament has so much in it that speaks to ordinary people at ordinary times trying to come to terms with the extraordinary fact of God, it's there that often the questions begin to be tackled.

Two hours into the New Year and we're talking about Joshua —chapter 3 to be precise! There's not many households doing that, I guess. But we start with Joshua because he was a man in the Bible who also passed a point like New Year and looked to the future. It was the day he led his people across the Jordan to an unknown land and to unknown times. And when he did so he acknowledged the uncertainty of it all, observing: 'You have not passed this way before'. And what was going to happen to them was as unknown then as the New Year is unknown to us. They, like we, had the past to remember, with everything that had happened for good or ill. They had been in the wilderness for more than a whole generation and sometimes it had seemed as if they would have been better off staying in Egypt, even if that had meant slavery. But now they were crossing the Jordan and you couldn't blame them if they were a touch anxious and a good deal excited. Joshua reminded them that they had not passed this way before. It was a new experience and there were new days to come, and on the edge of the unknown there was the same feeling of expectation as we ourselves have when we cross into a New Year.

And there was one thing that had seen them through their hardest times—and which Joshua was certain they would need to keep for times to come—and that was their faith in God who had brought them to this moment. Sometimes they found it hard to believe in him, just as some people today find it hard. It was like that when they were hungry and thirsty and the wilderness looked as though it was going to overwhelm them. But looking back on things, Joshua was absolutely convinced that God had always been there. And whatever was going to face them on the other side of the Jordan, God was still going to be there. He did not know the challenges that awaited. He was not sure of the possible difficulties of what they could be asked to do or face. He knew as little of tomorrow as we do on a New Year's morning. But he was sure of two things: first, that you don't hold back and become maudlin about yesterday; and second, that God doesn't suddenly pack up and leave you.

Many of them had had days when they had been afraid. They had been pretty low. And among the people there must have been some who were hesitant to pass to new experiences because, to use Rikki's word, their spirits were 'downbeat' and their faith was not up to it. But Joshua was not like that. And to help them there would be a visible symbol of the ark of the covenant. It could be something potent and evident. Wherever they went, God would go with them, marching step by step along the road. And the rest of that story is well enough known. It tells of how they went forward into the promised land. It talks of great days and grey days. It is the story of how, bit by bit, the tribes settled into a new land that would eventually become the cradle of the Son of God. It speaks of how they felt the hand of God among them, sometimes guiding, sometimes encouraging, sometimes correcting, sometimes very obvious, sometimes too hidden for their liking. But all the time it was there.

'And if you're wanting a glimpse into a New Year,' I said to Rikki, then that's the way it always has been for God's people. We haven't passed this way before. We don't know what lies beyond.

And there are some people who will cringe at the unknown and curl up in anxiety about what might come. And I'm sure you know that Christians can be just as introverted as anyone else.'

But before I went too far down the road of monologue, Rikki pulled me back to the present. The questions came again: 'What about now? ... What does it say to you about your Church? ... What are you trying to tell me about *me* and the things that affect me? ... I can see what you're saying about something new, but what does it really say about nineteen-ninety something?'

I thought for a moment. 'Well, if you're going to bring this idea right into the present, I think it makes us face up to these very questions about the Church and about ourselves. Take the Church. I remember hearing a sermon by the theologian Professor Tom Torrance some years ago in which he spoke of the Church being locked into a downward spiral. It was as if we too were in a wilderness and all we could do was look in on ourselves. We have become obsessed with facts and figures and statistics, while at the same time we go on closing down mission stations all over our country, either by a deliberate policy of the central Church or else by the guileless and loveless Gospel that, like the Revd I M Jolly, would only repel potential converts!'

Actually, I don't know if everyone would agree with Tom Torrance or not, but it would be foolish *not* to listen to him. There are many in the national Church, and indeed in local parishes, who are afraid of what Joshua would have called the Jordan and will risk nothing at all for the Kingdom of God. They won't risk ridicule and they won't risk danger because they have not passed these sorts of ways before and they are not so sure that they would ever want to. But this is exactly what faced Joshua.

Weren't there some then who said that it would be much better to have remained a slave in Egypt than to have been brought out into all the riskiness of this forlorn wilderness? These are the ones who in the New Year will do nothing. They will calculate the odds. They will present Christianity with a face of joylessness. They will go on speaking a lot about sin and very little about grace. They will turn from passing a new way and remain in the decreasing downward spiral so that they will not find new men and women for Christ, and not answer—not even *try* to answer— the sorts of questions that Rikki throws out so properly and so provocatively.

For me, I shall go on with a lot of my own brand of brinkman-ship and try new ways and be unafraid to rattle some of the weary old bones of a Church that can offer so much, but doesn't always make it.

'So,' I say to Rikki, 'go on asking your questions and I'll go on answering them!'

And there is more than the Church involved as we're talking into the early hours of the New Year, because I know too that Rikki wants to know about himself. Part of his search is to do with finding that happiness which will not be threatened or ended. Happiness is caught up in the unknown future with his home, his wife, his dogs. It is about these connections *not* being taken away.

I have to be honest enough to say that I certainly don't know it all. Ministers who claim to have all the answers are, to my mind, to be treated with suspicion. You cannot ever tell what the years are going to do for us and for those we love. All that we can say is that the weeks and months that are before us on this New Year will be similar in a lot of respects to the way we have already come so far. There will be days that are full of bright colours of happiness and success. And there will be other days that strike us because of their greyness and even their black. That's the way life is and it would be not only foolish, but also dishonest, to suggest that it is suddenly going to be different.

So I say to Rikki, 'Just because you are working your way towards the Christian faith, doesn't mean that you or I will possess some sort of immunity from the realities of life.'

But what I tell Rikki is that things are as true now as they were the day that Joshua crossed the Jordan and, for all that we don't know and *can't* know in advance, there is one thing that we *do* know—that as God has been with us in the past, he will be there with us tomorrow as well. And he will be there in strength and in love, not in weakness. And I'm not going to advertise a message of gloom. I won't tell him about personal hesitations or doubts as if they are some contemporary virtue. I know that he himself feels that the Church has risked far too often presenting itself with the face of 'I M Jolly'. And it's silly, because what we possess is the most glorious and the most hopeful and the most immovable treasure in Good News that will command tomorrow as much as it has commanded today.

I know it's not always as easy as we would like, to fit all the pieces of the picture together and understand what God is doing in our lives—any more than it was straightforward in Joshua's time. The challenge for any New Year is the challenge that we've had every year. We don't know, and I'm not going to pretend to know, what new experiences are waiting for us in this New Year. It would be silly to claim otherwise. But this much can be said: God stands as firmly secured in the future as he has been in our past. And in the future his nature and power will be absolutely the same as they have always been. Perhaps we shall have to face a tough time. But if we do, then God will be there with us and we shall not need to go through that tough time by ourselves. Indeed, we might find that this is going to be the greatest year we've had in a while—full of success and laughter and lots of good things. If that's so, then God will be among it with us as well, and it won't do any harm to say thank you.

'That's where you find this elusive thing called 'hope' in a New Year,' I tell Rikki.

And I really cannot offer him a single word more positive than that as we enter these days that neither of us has yet trod. I know he wants that to be so. I know that the search for hope and happiness is as precious to him as any part of the hunt for God. And even first thing in the New Year, we are down to the very basics of the questions that belong, I'm sure, to many people. And this talk of hope in a New Year is not illusory. There are some who would say it was. They would argue that it had no substance to it. They would claim that it's just a dream—a pipedream at that. But the evidence points the other way. And it is the evidence of our own lives for one. When you think of the years you've lived and the experiences you've had and the love you've enjoyed, do you honestly put these down to nothing more than a huge accident. All the things you've done, all the love you've received and given, all the creativity you've been part of, all the opportunities that have met—has it all just been a huge accident? There are some who will no doubt convince themselves that things are to be interpreted no more highly than that and you cannot argue with them. If someone wants to go through life believing that the body and the mind and the soul are only chance collisions of atoms, then there isn't much a minister or preacher can do to tell them otherwise. But I don't believe that and neither, I suspect, does Rikki Fulton, or else he wouldn't be so keen to find out.

I add, 'The way things have been with God in the world is the way things are going to be with God still. And that's why we can go into a New Year—or, indeed, into any sort of tomorrow—with a confidence that uncertainty is not finally going to overcome us. I'm not going to be dishonest and say that it's all going to be a bed of roses. I hope it is. But however it is, when the day or the

7

year draws to a close, God will have been with you. Perhaps we haven't walked this way before. But even if I don't know the road and what's round the next corner, I do know who is going to be there. And that gives me a lot of confidence.'

There was not a lot more to say—especially so late into the morning. But this last thought was still there. I had been thinking about a comment for the New Year in church and had been reading a few words of a writer called Emerson from his essay 'Work and Days'. I liked this message for New Year and I shared it that night with Rikki.

Live on tiptoe. Press on towards the goal. If you fall, fall forward. Make difficulty an incentive. Tell the people to go forward. Many things are right with the world. Nothing is accomplished which is not first begun. New Year is the portal to the land of beginning again. Life is a grand adventure in which faith is the supreme necessity. Write it on your heart that every day is the best of the year.

That's upbeat enough, isn't it? I imagine 'Jolly' wouldn't have said anything like this, would he? If he fell forward, he'd fall on his face.

'If you or I fall forward in this year or any other, Rikki,' I tell him—'it will be into the arms of a God who will never desert us and, ultimately, never let us down.'

2

By Influence and Example

RIKKI Fulton is a prolific writer. It is not only in the area of comedy that his talents are to the forefront. I have shared with him many conversations centred on what is clearly a work which has given him much pleasure, a lot of sifting, and a great deal of personal reflection—his autobiography. And one of the areas of discussion we have had, has centred on the many and varied influences and examples that have confronted both of us as we grew into adulthood and developed the sort of interests and careers which we have pursued.

Our shared experiences led me one dark February day to consider the personal influences in our lives and how much they shape us into the sort of people we become. As a starting point, we can do no better than to look at the life of our own Saviour and see if there was anything specific in his experiences which contributed to his own enormous influence on our world, both in his own time and ever since.

There are a few pointers in the Bible. One of these is in Luke's Gospel, where we learn of Jesus at home with his parents 'growing and becoming strong, filled with wisdom' (Luke 2:52). But generally there's a huge silence which spans long years in his life. We all celebrate the birth of Jesus in Bethlehem with its related stories which become central to the pageant of nativity celebrations. And we also know that, as a man of about thirty, he came into Galilee, in Mark's words, preaching the Gospel of God. But between these points there is virtually nothing. God was alive as flesh and blood and nobody appeared to know about it.

Shepherds in the hills had their memories and nothing more. Wise men in the East had apparently gone home again and stayed silent. There had perhaps even been another census since Jesus was born, and who's to say that maybe the same folk had searched for yesterday's ghosts in Bethlehem's streets and stables. But it all belonged to the past and only the next generation of innkeeper and revellers was the same—still preoccupied by the same important things as on that night when the star was in the sky and it sounded as if heaven was singing a song of glory to earth below.

And whatever else that lay in between could almost be guess-work—but not all of it. For there's an odd snatch, here and there, as in Luke's Gospel, where we can see something of what was going on to shape Jesus' life for the great things that were waiting to be done. Mary and Joseph, faithful to God and to the faith of their fathers, were raising their son to know God. They were bringing him up as a healthy youngster. They were attentive to his education and were thrilled, I'm sure, not only with his ability, but also with his wisdom—not always one and the same thing.

For our Lord Jesus Christ—as for Rikki, myself and for *all* of us—there were personal influences of great power that made Him ready to do the great work which has so captivated mankind for two thousand years. It was not by accident that Jesus was ready to do God's work. It didn't happen without a weight of example, of love, of care and patience. And when Jesus eventually came into Galilee preaching the Gospel of God, he did it on the foundation of years of preparation, years of influence and example.

And surely, if we ever want to write our own autobiography we have to do the same. We can write about influences and examples in the past, probably from home and family. And certainly, we can look back across the years and know that whatever we have done, and however we have done it, it has been shaped (I would argue) by God, and (Rikki and I would agree) by parents, the wider family, good friends, school, the Forces, and so on. But where we are today, and how we came to be here, is not an accident.

All of us can point to someone and say, 'But for him or her, but for that bit of guidance there, but for that timely word, but for that support and love given when it was most needed, but for any or all of these, I would not be who I am today, nor could I have achieved whatever it is that people believe I have achieved.' And if we look at Jesus Christ, then we have to say that God left the formative years in the hands of Mary and Joseph. They loved him and taught him and inspired him and, I'm sure where necessary, they corrected him. And because of their influence and example, a Saviour was prepared who was fit to do the work his Father had sent him to do.

Instances of this sort of influence are widespread. One of the gem's of our own literature is Robert Burns' poem 'The Cotter's Saturday Night'. Surely the image of influence which is the poem's chief glory is of the cotter, on a Saturday night, before the blazing fire, taking down the great family Bible and reading from its pages to the silent attentive listeners. It was the stuff of which 'Scotia's grandeur was made'—that influence of faith in which God's word was so alive. It made us one of the great missionary nations of the world, far beyond our meagre numbers, and through people like David Livingstone and Graham of Kalimpong and many many more, the vitality of faith was taken all over the world.

Then Rikki and I began to look at more recent times and how, all around us, there are people who do great things and inspire marvellous moments by their sheer influence. Communism was stripped out of Europe not by the violence of war which had been the lifelong fear of people born after the Second World War, but by the example of great people who would not be broken by its grip. Andrei Sakharov in the former Soviet Union: brave Christian priests in Poland: a young pastor in the hill country of Romania—their examples of courage and their influence of integrity not only moved whole nations in the end, but was part of the excising from the world a repressive creed that dragged people down into the very depths of misery.

Or, nearer home, we remembered the example and influence and formative work of a man like the evangelist Tom Allan in Glasgow. It was a love which touched lots of people, and not only touched them, but succeeded in changing direction for people and recreating for them hope out of darkness. And now, years after his untimely death, his work goes on because people are moved by that sort of compassion and by that sort of love and by the overriding compulsion of its originator, Jesus Christ.

But if that's what the recent past tells us, and if we can enjoy searching for ourselves the influences that have shaped our *own* lives, then we have to go a step further. I'm not so sure we can sit back with biographical contentment without seeing in this area of example and influence some sort of challenge for today— simply because we have to recognise that if we have had influences on us in the past, we are, whether we like it or not, people whose lives today will bear influence on others too. Imagine what it would have been like had Jesus stopped; if, after all those wonderful formative persuasions, he slipped through adulthood and ended up doing nothing; if the conclusion had been that he possessed an attitude that said, with a degree of personal smugness, 'I'm alright, but the rest of you will have to learn for yourselves'.

It's a bit like that other biographical moment in the New Testament when two men are described, each of them going into church to pray. One of them was so self satisfied that every example and every influence in his life had shaped him into perfection. He didn't have any of the sins and errors of other people, and he thanked God for making him so different. But the other was just as aware, I'm sure, of the various gifts he had received in past years from other people. He was very sensitive to the issues of life and how they ought to be handled. He knew that a lot of what he did and said was not matching up to the example which had been set by the many people who moulded him. And because of that, what he said was different too: 'God be merciful to me a sinner'.

And when we think about ourselves, whether we are writing an autobiography or whether we are just trying to sort out our lives, we have a choice. We can either be smug about how good we are. Don't forget that out Scottish heritage, particularly in religion, has known quite a lot of that sort of attitude—you only have to read Robert Burns' poem 'Holy Willie's Prayer' to know just how smug we can actually be. It speaks of a terrible influence and a shocking example—and, what's worse, it's an attitude still found in a number of Christians today. They are the grim-faced purveyors of self-righteousness who repel thousands around them by their counsel of hypocritical perfection. And their influence and example in our own times, when thousands are searching for honest answers in faith, is one of the factors that drive people away from the Church more than anything else ....

Alternatively, we can be aware of all the good that others have tried to instil in us in the past and, knowing that, continue to wish, despite our imperfections, to set some sort of caring, loving, understanding example in our own day. And our influence could be huge. Our example could be critical. And we certainly cannot begin to call ourselves Christians if we do not face up to such a head-on challenge.

This discussion between Rikki and myself began to centre on our own lives and the possible details that matter to us in the sifting of our experiences. Suddenly a lot of issues dealing with our *present* and *future* began to emerge, just as much as our past— and it became a bit of a challenge.

Here I am, a preacher and teacher, with some sort of public place given to me in which to mould opinions and lives. Here is Rikki Fulton, with a wider public still who are captivated by what he offers as a professional actor in today's media-orientated world. Doesn't all this present us with some sort of challenge?

Take the young generation these days. The power of influence and example on the young now is so diverse and complex as to make their way in life all the harder compared to previous generations. When many of us look back to our earlier adult lives, we can see that many things were far more cut and dried than they are now. The influences and examples were pretty obvious. They were often based on some form of basic Christian understanding of life. And what made them all the more appealing was the fact that they were comparatively simple. It was easy to tell right from wrong and you were fairly well guided in the right direction. It's not like that now. For one thing, the whole underlying philosophy of education in schools is no longer a Christian one. Young people are being brought up towards adulthood with the impression that there is a number of religions which embrace parts of the truth, some of the truth, and together all of the truth. At the same time society is offering them a whole range of new idols; while the media frequently portrays the immoral as the moral.

And so while people like Rikki and myself wonder about past influences and how they have moulded us, we have, at the same time, to be sensitive to the type of influence and example we offer today. We have to be patient to listen. We have to take time to understand the forces that are tugging the young this way and that. We have to be unafraid, particularly if we are men and women in Christ, to set the example of what we say we believe.

But what is even more important is that we do it with the best face of Christianity. And I say that because in a world which is searching for faith, in a society like ours which looks from time to time to see if the Church has any word or input that really matters, people will not be satisfied with the grim caricature of Jesus Christ that so many Christians represent in word and in lifestyle. Christian influence has nothing to do with pettiness and gossip. It should not try to tailor its faith to suit outdated behaviour. It should not do the world down as often as it does —as if God had set us here to be miserable and, if we are not, then something has to be far wrong.

It's a terrible face for the Church to offer. But to take the opposite view, wherever we are, we have an example of open and exciting, uninhibited Christian love to offer: that love which long ago was described as being patient and kind, not riven with envy, respecting other men and women, and loving every new day on which you awake. If we set that sort of example, who can tell what could be achieved for Christ now.

Mary and Joseph set a good example in their own home with their son. And thus they prepared the Saviour of the world for the task he was to undertake. It gives rather fine nuance to the phrase 'entertaining angels unawares'. But we too can do it. Indeed we *have* to do it—every day by the way we talk and think and act. It's great to look back on many good and varied influences. But what will be looked back on as our example and our influence? Forget the grim and stuffy Christianity that has no place now. Forget it and entertain *today's* angels unawares.

3

The Final Enemy

I N a deeply reflective interview on BBC television some years ago, Rikki Fulton was asked what his view of heaven might be. His answer was personal and honest: 'Heaven,' he said, 'if there *is* a heaven, would be where I can continue to enjoy my home, the love and company of my wife, and the presence of my dogs!'

It is scarcely the answer that belongs to a theological purist, but then the answer that the theological purist might give would not necessarily speak much sense to many of us. But there is no doubt at all that one of the most fundamental religious questions of all concerns the fact of death. For many people, Rikki and myself included, the intrusion of death is a brooding threat which lurks in the background as a challenge we appear to be able to do very little about.

This is yet another of these questions of faith which, as a parish minister, is never very far away—and yet is not often directly raised by members of the Church.

'Tell me,' Rikki said to me, 'can the Christian faith prove to me that death can be defeated? Is there anything you can say that will take the enormous fear of death away from me?'

It takes courage to ask a direct question like this, and I am sure many others want some answers too.

I think it might be true that the more you love life, the more you command life, the more you put into life—the more you are resistant to the thought that one day it is inevitable that life will be stripped away from you.

And so it seems to me that when anyone is ready to ask these very deep questions, it is right that the issue should not be avoided, but addressed with every vestige of faith and honesty which, as a minister, you may possess.

There is no doubt that if, as a minister, you try to face up to that sort of question, then the sort of answer you have must centre on the one man who in the history of the world has faced up to death and has defeated it—Jesus Christ.

Good Friday was only a week or two away when Rikki and I had another discussion on this subject, and it was all the more clear to me that we ministers have to address what the message of Good Friday and its death actually means, as honestly as we proclaim the fact of Easter's resurrection.

Remember the signs that followed the death of Jesus Christ, as they are reported in the New Testament. Just before they happened, there was a loud cry from Jesus—'Into Thy Hands I commit my Spirit. It is finished'. And then he died. The soldiers went back down the hill to their barracks, and Mary and John and a few other people who had remained to the end, moved silently from the cross, distraught at what they had seen.

At the same time, think of Pilate saying, 'Thank God! Thank God it's all over with!' And I imagine that if our Lord's last words were reported to him, and in particular that last cry of 'It is finished', then Pilate might at last have found himself agreeing with the man he had condemned, but never properly understood. It certainly must have been Pilate's wish for this whole unfortunate episode to be finished. He had ordered Christ's death because there seemed to be no other way to deal with the trouble. And even though he had given every appearance of being totally in control of the situation, the whole affair had made him feel uneasy. Even if it were now all finished, he had been uneasy enough beforehand still to want to make sure. He ordered the guard commander to keep a special watch on Jesus' tomb.

I suppose that Caiaphas and Annas, the Jewish leaders, also said, 'Thank God'. Thank God that things were settled now and they were rid of that meddlesome disturber of the peace. It was all over. And, for the first time, they might have agreed unwittingly with something Jesus himself had said—for it to be finished, was all that they had ever wanted. Three long years they had been agitated by the man, now it was all over—and what a wonderful relief to know that religion was safely back in their own hands, rescued from this spiritual deviant.

It was also possible that the ordinary people said, 'Thank God'. Thank God that things were clear again and they could possess all the timid certainties that belong to those who have no imagination. It was safe to know what was what and who was in charge. And even if it had been a bit exciting to be on this roller-coaster of religion with Christ, it was probably better now that they knew where they stood. You can cope with no hope if you know there is none to hope for.

So Jesus died. You might say that he was forsaken and, in the end, had been truly abandoned. You might want to argue that what Calvary tells us is that good people can try their best and visionaries can have their day but, finally, the ways of the world will win. And you could go on to add that Pilate was right and Caiaphas was right and Annas was right and the people were right. Maybe even Peter had been right when, at the last, he didn't want to know Jesus.

The world will have its way. You will live for a time and then you will die and it's as simple as that, because mankind controls its own destiny and you simply have to make the best of a bad job.

'That's pretty depressing,' interrupted Rikki, 'if that's *all* you can say!'

I hurriedly reassured him, 'It's not the *final* word. However clearcut it looked then, and however clearcut it might look now, it's not the final word.'

But I know that you have to be careful. There are some, even from within the Christian faith, who try to be a bit too clever. They say that you have to distinguish between Good Friday and Easter. Good Friday is Man's day. It is the day when humanity showed its ultimate capacity to do what it wanted. Then, they say, Easter is God's day, and it's a better and stronger and more hopeful day because it is the triumphant day.

In some respects this is a good distinction for some; but I don't particularly like it, because I don't think it's really true. We cannot abandon Good Friday to mankind. We cannot even hint that God wasn't totally in control of things on Good Friday. We cannot believe that Jesus appealed to his Father in prayer and there was nothing but impotent silence echoing back at him. We cannot accept that the God of history was *removed* from history, even if only for a day. For if that were so, if that's what happened, then the next question to ask would be, 'When next *did* it happen? When next *will* it happen? What catastrophe will God's next absence portend?'

But look rather at the signs that followed our Lord's death. The skies darkened and the thunder rolled above and a centurion looked up and really believed it when he said, 'Truly this was the Son of God'. And then in staggering words that belong to all the Gospel writers, except John, 'The curtain of the Temple was torn in two from top to bottom'. It was a curtain which for centuries had hidden the heart of God from the gaze of the on-looker—so conclusively hidden God that it was a curse to the people. It was there to shut people out. It was a warning to sinful men and women that where the last mysteries of religion were concerned, they should keep a respectful distance. On the other hand, it also shut God in. For behind the hanging veil there was a silence as deep as death itself, and a darkness as black as night. It had hung there for years and looked as though it could go on hanging forever. And now, as the thunder crashed above and the clouds rolled in to veil a city which had thought it had closed out God's final efforts to reveal his love, the curtain was split wide open from top to bottom. Note that it was from the top, from the place where no man would or could begin. It was split from heaven to earth. And it was split by God himself.

Good Friday does not lie outside God's ultimate control at all. He didn't want Jesus to die. You would be a fool to think he did, because God never wants to see pain or suffering or injustice. He had sent Jesus to promote love and offer forgiveness. But when humanity had done its worst, at the very moment Jesus died, God was there and God was saying, 'But I'm still here right in the middle of death, and I still love, and I split this curtain wide open for you today so that at last you can see me as I am'.

For all of us, there is no verse in the Bible that has the potential for so much hope and promise as this one: 'The curtain of the Temple was torn in two from top to bottom'.

And what Rikki's question reminds us is that the curtain is still being erected. And because of this, so many questions are not answered. In our world there remains such a lot of agony. There is a turmoil of injustice that torments people in so many places. There is a veil that hides dignity and hope from people. There are barriers to men and women being reconciled to each other. There is a divide between rich and poor. And there are all the honest questions about living and dying that go on and on being left unanswered.

And so perhaps we still wonder—could Pilate have been right

and isn't the world a more powerful place than God can handle? Could Caiaphas and Annas have been right, and isn't it better just to have a religion that keeps people right with laws and morals, rather than tempting them with wild notions of salvation and new life? And could the ordinary folk have been right too and aren't they right still if the rollercoaster of Christianity is honestly nothing more than a wild fling with no foundation in common sense?

And we wonder all the more when we see Calvary, or its like, happening still in our midst. Every time a terrorist bullet cuts down an innocent man or woman or child—Jesus is crucified. Every time a person is degraded for his colour—Jesus is crucified. Every time a person dies of hunger in this world of plenty—Jesus is crucified. Every time we compromise or fall short of our best deliberately—Jesus is crucified. Every time a man or woman weeps for the death of a partner or a child—Jesus is crucified. And yet none of these is the last word. They are not the last word simply because of Good Friday. The veil is still being rent apart today to show us the love of God stooping into our world to try to answer these questions and these situations which so quickly devastate people.

However much the veil is erected today and however many people there might be who are all too ready to write God off, the veil is ripped open and God's love shows through once more.

Studdert Kennedy is a poet I like very much. He was a padre in the army and bore the message of Jesus Christ to those who suffered the four long years of misery on the Great War's western front. There is nowhere this century, and surely very few places in history, where the eclipse of God might have looked more apparent—and where the re-enactment of Good Friday was a daily event. It must have been a shocking veil. It was a veil that hid God's love from men who must have winced at the distant memory of what love had once meant to them. It must have evoked every one of the questions that so many of us ask. The padre who went through Calvary day after day had the eyes to see the veil being torn open while everything else was so black. And the love that shone through for Good Friday, safe in the hands of God, can always look three days ahead. For one of the things you see behind the veil is the sun rising in an Easter Garden. This is what Studdert Kennedy said in his poem 'Truth' (from *The Rhymes of G A Studdert Kennedy*, Hodder & Stoughton, 1927):

> *God sleeps or is he dead? And all that we have read of his great love, a lie that must be buried with others in the past. The last—the very last, sweet lie we shall ever have—to keep us from despair, which is the truth, the cruel truth.*
>
> *More light. More light. O God of life, one breath of air, or else we die. The shadows conquer, and we lie in darkness, darkness of despair, which is the second death.*
>
> *But look. The shadows weaken, and the sun breaks through. 'Tis true. God lives. I knew ... I think I always knew.*

I will die. And so will all of us. You cannot pretend it away. You must face up to it. Calvary happens. But God reigns—I believe it with all my heart—God reigns. The veil is opened up. And if you are ready to look you can still see him.

It is not finished. It is not finished when you die. And who's to say that behind the veil you do not see your home and your wife ... oh, yes, and your dogs too.

4

Keep on trying

Easter Monday

I DON'T know how often I've encouraged Rikki—or is it *dis*couraged him—with these few words: 'Keep on. Don't give up'. For a man who has such an exciting mind, the greatest frustration of all with the Christian faith is that he is so keen to have answers, and the answers in faith appear to come a good sight slower than anywhere else. In fact, he freely confesses to have given up for a while, when he reconciled himself to life as an atheist. There are no answers apparently and, if that's so, then it seemed wiser to Rikki for many years to stop the torment of searching, and to get on with his life the way things are. Certainly for a long time it worked, as it has worked and still works for others. But not altogether. For here he was again, really searching for the answers that matter. And like so many others, he needs to be encouraged by the Church; he needs to be treated honestly; he needs to believe that what he is asking is neither too simple or too silly; encouragement is needed now—and not the promise of an appointment for a chat at some later date!

One of the great touches of humanity in the Bible is that we find it filled with men and women who needed exactly the same. All the way through the Bible you come across people who have hoped for things, or worked for things, or prayed for things which, in the end, look as if they have not happened. It is about the silence of faith and the frustration of faith. And if it troubles Rikki Fulton like many others today, it caused just as much trouble in biblical times too.

King David was one of the greatest kings Israel ever had. He took a small nation, driven with factions and cliques and opposing forces, and in a dominant reign manufactured a golden age when Israel blossomed and expanded and found a security she had never had before and would never have again. He seemed to have the Midas touch, so that whatever he wanted fell into place. It was a staggering life from teenage years spent looking after sheep in the hills of Judah, dreaming his dreams, writing his poetry—through to the end when he passed on to his son Solomon the throne of a major Middle Eastern power. But just before any of us feel a touch envious of David, let us recall that it was not always so easy.

The man who looked as though he could achieve whatever he willed, almost at the drop of a hat, was thwarted in his dearest ambition of all—to construct a Temple on Zion that would be a fit place to worship the God in whom he strongly believed and whose hand he saw written large through the history of his fathers. Conquering lesser nations was no bother; prosperity in abundance for his people was a mark of his time; organising even the baser ambitions of his heart through the lustful acquisition of Bathsheba and the murder of her husband Uriah, all fell into place for David; and writing poetry of such excellence that even today his work is the foundation of the worship of God's people —this again was no problem. But as far as this one building was concerned, David died with the dream unfulfilled and the prayers, it seemed, unanswered.

It was Solomon, his son, who was left to do it. And when it was completed, Solomon gathered the people together for the official opening. It was a grand affair and Solomon, in his speech, reminded the people that it was his late father's dream that they now saw in reality. They had heard him talking about it, but for one reason or another it had not been possible. And in a poignant moment of recollection, Solomon reminded the people in these words:

> *The Lord said to David my father, 'Whereas it was in your heart to build a house for my name, you did well that it was in your heart. Nevertheless you shall not build the house, but your son who shall be born to you shall build the house for my name'.*
>
> ~ 1 Kings 8:18-19 ~

It was a good and honourable thing for David to want to do it. It was a noble dream. It was a vision that would not be put off forever. Nevertheless, it would not happen for David, but would happen finally through his son. We can add up all the rest that David did and reckon him as Israel's greatest ever king, but here his dream was defeated, his hope crushed, and he did not see what most he wanted.

Or what about the men who centuries later walked the road to Emmaus that first Easter Day? Don't we think that they too had a similar sense of frustration about their hopes and dreams? They had been with Jesus Christ, had listened to him, had been bold enough to hope and believe that someone at last had come who was going to make religion live and allow it to be sensible for ordinary people with ordinary hearts and minds. But now Jesus was dead and, as they talked with the stranger on the road that day, they showed a terrible disappointment together with a deep-seated frustration. 'We had hoped,' they said—bravely hoped, eagerly hoped, longingly and anxiously hoped—'that this was the man to redeem Israel.' They had hoped for it then, and there are scores of people today who would hope for it now. But a cross on Calvary pointed to failure and looked as though these men then were going to be left to pick up the pieces and get on with life without him.

And it was the same with a man like Paul. He took the great message of Christ's love to the city of Rome, where he hoped and dreamed of winning the hearts of his fellow citizens with such a commanding message, but instead he found the same rejection that once had befallen his Master. Later in history, beyond biblical times, it was the same with the theologian Martin Luther. He never wanted to split the Church in two; he never sought a reputation as a wild revolutionary—he simply wished to see the Church back on the rails again. And as the years slipped by, he gradually came to see that, frustratingly, it could not happen like that.

It is the same for ordinary people at any time. Maybe they stand on the edge of a crisis and they get down on their knees and pray to God—perhaps for the first time in years. They may have spent a long time indifferent to God, but suddenly something is sparked off inside them and communion with God becomes critically important. But what they hoped to avert from themselves, or from someone they love, comes, as it were, inexorably to pass, and souls who have been driven in despair to the throne of God depart, wondering where in Creation this God is who has so stunned them with his silence.

Whatever the time, and wherever the place, and whoever the person—we are at the centre of the questions that the likes of Rikki Fulton and a thousand others ask and keep on asking: 'Where are the answers? ... Is there any point in keeping on? ... What does it all mean? ... How can we ever begin to have confidence in a God who treats us like this? ... What justice is there in religion? ... What's the point?' For, like David of old, you have it in your heart to do something, or say something, or offer something, or search for something—and it is good that it is in your heart. God has said so. Nevertheless it shall not be. And you are left wondering what this frustration is all about and if there are any answers at all. Perhaps you even begin to doubt the minister who tells you to 'Keep on trying'.

I can only try to find the answer in the Old and New Testaments—the answer to spiritual frustration and thwarted aims. And the uniform evidence of how to handle difficult moments like these is an encouragement to hold onto the dream and retain the vision. For if we examine the history of faith, then whatever is good and positive and worthwhile about that faith comes to fulfilment in the providence of God. David did not see the Temple. For one reason or another it was not left to him to bring it about. But the vision he had was not lost. It did not disappear with him when he died. The vision of the Temple, as a crucial and integral place for the worship of God's people, came most marvellously into being during the reign of Solomon.

The two men on the Emmaus Road, pained to the depths of their hearts that Jesus had been crucified, were not left disappointed. Perhaps the path to salvation was strewn with greater pain than they had envisaged. Perhaps the Cross had never looked to them to be a suitable vehicle for salvation. Perhaps they could not understand the way that God was working. But the experience that was round the corner for them on that glorious Easter Day was something far beyond what they could have wished, even in their wildest dreams. For Easter came. The world was entering its most exciting era. And they were to be among its first reporters.

Paul thought he would capture Rome with his preaching. And when he reached the city, of which he was a long-standing citizen, it must have been a terrible shock to him that the Church existed and was compelled to exist in the catacombs and rat-ridden sewers of the city. It was a crushing disappointment as sometimes you can detect in his letters. And it was an experience which for Paul would end in imprisonment and execution. But the Gospel he preached to Rome was to have a far greater victory than he could ever have foreseen. Within two and a half centuries not only the people of Rome were touched by the Gospel news, but even the emperor himself, in a moment of dedication, knelt down and committed his life to Jesus Christ. What was in Paul's heart was good and noble and, if it did not happen for him in his own lifetime, it happened for him and through him and because of him nonetheless.

And it's the same for all of us—Rikki, me or you. The Bible pleads with us to hold on to the dreams and visions of faith. In the Church, for example, wherever we worship, it would be a poor and tawdry thing if we did not have the courage to dream dreams any more. The Old and New Testaments cry out to us to recapture what sometimes, I believe, we are in danger of losing. Have a vision of the city of God in our midst. Work for the salvation of souls. Dream of the day that your friends and neighbours, together with your very family, will fall in love with Jesus, as in your own heart you are in love with him—and the Kingdom of God will inch forward that little bit more. And yet, as we do it, frustrations will still come. Crippling frustrations such as the Church getting lost, as sometimes it does, in the muddle of social trivia and moral duplicity. Or the frustration that comes from having such a burning love for God inside you and yet you don't appear able to pass it on to other people, and especially to the people you love most. And that is when you say, 'Keep on trying'.

We all remember that great twentieth century preacher of God's Word, Martin Luther King. He was a man whose life pulsed with a message of love and peace and justice; who, in an unforgettable speech, told a worldwide audience of a dream he had. And soon afterwards, for some inexplicable reason, he was cut down by an assassin's bullet. Was it wrong for him to dream? Was it a false thing for him to have in his heart the ambition that men and women are born free, should live free, and have no barrier of colour or background to hinder them in the living of this marvellous gift of life itself? And if it is false, then Paul was false and Christ was false and the whole thrust of the Christian message is false. But this noble vision and dream was in his heart and was not rendered futile because it did not happen in his own life-time. For there are signs all the time that the dream is nearer. And none of us has a right to give up on the vision that the Bible gives us, whatever our generation or society.

Then again, it is maybe we ourselves who have the dream for somebody we love or for ourselves. It's not wrong to hope for the best, or to work for the best, or to pray for the best. It's not wrong, because if lives cannot be lived at their highest and most productive, then they are being lived at a level below that for which they were created. It might be that in our own experience, there are times when things don't turn out as we have envisaged or wished. The cold intrusion of death cuts across lives, young and old, to shout out a seeming denial of every dream we have been harbouring. But it doesn't make the dream wrong. It doesn't invalidate our hopes any more than the dream of Cleopas and his friend on the Emmaus Road was to be seen to be invalid.

Then again, there will be times when we don't understand, times when there is no rhyme nor reason to what has hit us, times when we are deeply stunned. But it does not mean the end, it does not invalidate God's love, and it does not point to a wildly indiscriminate world in which there is ultimately no hand of God to be seen which might work for the final victory of good.

It is good that these things are in our heart. God forbid the day when noble visions and great thoughts and godly dreams cease to matter. God forbid the day when, in ordinary life, men and women stop seeking the extraordinary. And if there is any sort of challenge to us as one day succeeds another, it is that none of us becomes inured to the trivial or tawdry. That is not to say there will never be times when the dream does not come to pass, when the vision does not become concrete, when ambitions are thwarted, when people are not told, 'Nevertheless, you shall not build'.

But there will never be a time either when what is good, true, honest and lovely can be so buried as never to rise again. That is the underpinning assertion which alone begins to offer an answer to the frustrations of life and faith. It is part of the Church's most urgent and treasured possessions. Because I believe it, I want to say to people like Rikki, to *any* who will listen, 'Keep on trying'.

It was Alfred Lord Tennyson, who wrote the following familiar lines in his poem 'In Memoriam', maybe as familiar as some parts of the Bible itself: 'It is better to have loved and lost than never to have loved at all'. In a sense these are holy words. It is better to have loved and lost, better to have worked and not seen the fruit, better to have dreamed and not seen with our own eyes, better to have had a vision and not beheld than never to have loved or worked or dreamed or had vision at all. That is better as an inspiration to life than a vacuous, timid nothing.

It does no service to people for Christianity to breast-beat its doubts. Our faith is about certainties; certainties of life, certainties in death, certainties in eternity. It is good that these great thoughts and enterprises are with us. Things *will* happen, but sometimes at a place and time beyond what we imagine. But better all of them in their God-appointed hour, than none of them at all. And because of this unconquerable faith, because the Church has the right every day to walk the Emmaus Road with Jesus Christ; even if we don't immediately recognise him, disappointment and fear need never drag us down again.

'So, I'm not ashamed to say it, my good friend, *Keep on trying!*'

5

Ghosts?

WHY doesn't the Church explain better the things it believes? Why must people be told that faith is so hard? Doctrines might be clear in your mind, but they are not always clear to people who are ordinary seekers after truth. And when Rikki speaks to me in that fashion, he issues a challenge on behalf of the 'ordinary punter' with which I instantly identify.

Sometimes we chat together about our childhood days and the things we did and heard and believed then. I remembered, for example, my fear, the fear of a ten year old who had been told of the Holy Ghost. There were no explanations other than the statement that this particular 'ghost' was everywhere and surrounded us day and night. It is a very basic doctrine of the Church and yet, so starkly presented, conjured images of a white-sheeted figure with slit eyes and a halo about its head, hovering threateningly outside the bedroom window. It is just one example of the lack of clarity and lack of sympathy in some of our 'churchspeak' which took me through years of teenage alienation from Christianity and which took Rikki through twenty-five years of resignation to near atheism.

So let's take this 'ghost' from the past, perhaps one of the most difficult doctrines of the Church, and let us see if there is any way at all we can begin to speak together of a Holy Ghost, or a

Holy Spirit in a way that might not be in the traditional imagery of the Church, but which might begin to touch the mind and, through the mind, the soul in a fashion that makes some sense.

With Rikki's acting background, we began our chat in his domain, with one of the great epic films of the century, *Gone with the Wind.* If we could take it beyond the romance between Scarlett O'Hara and Rhett Butler, we could then begin to discover much more in the novel and the film.

The story is about everything being uprooted in the terrible events of a Civil War. Whatever the justice of the causes on either side, you cannot help but feel sympathy with the people all over the Union and in the Confederate States whose lives were being ripped apart. It is the story of things 'going with the wind'. Like some great hurricane unleashed not only on the land, but let loose to devastate love and hope and dreams and security, it became a wind before which no one could stand erect and untouched. It bent everybody. It destroyed not just old ways, but also people—even some of the people it tried to touch with benevolence. And in the end, so much was changed, so much could no longer be the same ever again.

That is the effect of a wind which can sweep across a country to wreak its own particular physical and emotional havoc. And it's an effect to which all of us can respond, and to which we can, in part, understand. It is like the 'wind of change' which the politician Harold MacMillan once foresaw sweeping across the whole continent of Africa. And how awesomely accurate his vision of the future proved to be.

But there is another description of wind which takes me back to these old 'ghosts'—it is the wind which the Bible cares to speak of in its description of this mysterious and awkward element of our faith. They were all together in a room and the sound came to them 'like the rush of a mighty wind' (Acts 2:2). It filled the room where they were sitting. It filled the whole house. There was no escaping it. Everywhere there was wind—commanding everything in its path—and in its arrival, whipping before it what seemed to be tongues of fire, people spoke in all sorts of languages that let them tell of Jesus Christ to whoever would listen. It seemed to be the realisation of Jesus' promise not to leave men and women without help in coming to know God. And the most surprising thing about it was that, menacing as it might have looked and sounded, those who were present appeared to sense that it was marked with love and shot through with benevolence. There was nothing malicious, nothing that would make a ten year old tremble at night for fear of the unknown!

When God in his Spirit breathed among the people, it was a breath of love. It was quite unlike the wind which tore away so much in the Civil War between the American States, quite unlike the winds or war and winds of passion and winds of change which we find neither easy nor accommodating. The wind of the Holy Spirit is good and I suppose we ought to try to see if there is any parallel to draw for our own times.

The first lesson for us to take to ourselves is that the Holy Spirit came to be a personal gift for people. He was universal. He was not locked into a room and confined to these few who happened to be there at the time. He was for everybody. He was for Peter and Andrew. He was for all the disciples. He was for men and women of every nation who were in Jerusalem that day. He was for every generation. He is for me, and for anyone else at all who is wanting to listen to and feel for and wonder about the truth of Almighty God. And that's the way Jesus was too, of course. He was for *all* people. Perhaps one of the greatest mistakes that certain elements in the Church commit today is to downplay this wide universal scope of the grace of Jesus Christ. He was for *all* people. Look at his life and ministry and see how much more expansive it was than we sometimes allow our Church to be. He was for the poor. He championed the downtrodden. But that didn't mean, by definition, that he excluded the rich from his loving influence. Look at the compassion he had for Joseph of Arimathaea and for Nicodemus—and for the rich young man as well. He was also for the simple, but did not despise the clever. He responded to those who were open with their emotions, but had a good affection for the dour folk in life, as a man like Peter sometimes was. He had an abiding passion for the sinner and he knew that his life's work was to do something to make salvation a personal gift for them, but he also respected the good and honest in society, seeing in them the sorts of people who could be very beneficial in building the Kingdom of God. That is the way it was with our Lord who breathed life and energy into our world.

But, sadly, it's not like that in the Church. We love to pigeon-hole people. We feel we have to do God's work for him and are especially ready to separate the sheep from the goats. We take the message of Pentecost—and we say, 'No, not there. This wind cannot blow there. We will not allow it to blow there'.

God's Holy Spirit is not for the rich, we hear said. Condemn them. Tell them, as once was said, that wealthy people have a one way ticket to hell. Don't even think about the good that wealth can do, but concentrate on the bad you often imagine it is achieving. Just say that God loves the poor and therefore the Holy Spirit will not breathe on the rich. Or again, God's Spirit is not for the good. Laugh at their goodness. Despise what is dismissed as middle-class morality. For God loves the sinner; and the better and wilder your sins have been, the more chance you have of being loved and saved. And God's Spirit is not for the wise. Some people can be too clever by half and it's wonderful to pull them down from their lofty heights. Better to be simple and God will reach you much more easily.

There is a great deal of good in the Church today and we should not be slow to say it. There are many signs that the Holy Spirit is actively alive in a lot of our work. But still we sometimes manage to put good honest folk down. It is better to toe the line, to put down the rich, to decry those whose politics do not pass the test of trendiness, to mock innovators and to decide that the Holy Spirit has no place among them. But that is not how I read the New Testament. That is not what the day of Pentecost appears to tell me. This mighty, embracing universal wind of God touched all folk then, just as it might touch anyone today who is ready to stand out in the open, face up to it, and be counted.

The second lesson about the wind of God is that the Holy Spirit is singularly identified with love. He is unlike the wind which was so devastating as it swept away what was so precious in the life and love of America's North and South. The breath of the Holy Spirit is a breath of love. It was the same breath of love which made this world into a Garden of Eden for men and women to experience at first hand what God's gift could be like. It was the same breath of love which created life in the valley of dry bones. It was the same breath of love which spoke generously in Jesus Christ of forgiveness through a Cross and new life through resurrection. These are the evidences of that wind of God. Strong and mighty and universal—and it is a *wind of love*. And again we need to emphasise that today. We need to do this because there still can be a lot in our world, and in our Church, which is carping and unloving.

We can start in our own home. We need to start with a love for those who love us. We need to start in the home of the Church with a love for those who share the good news of Jesus Christ with us. We need to start with a neighbour, perhaps with the neighbour we find especially difficult. We need to start in these sorts of places because, if we cannot catch the fire of love there, then it will be a fire we are quite incapable of spreading any further. But such a spread is what is required. So often we have tried to terrorise people into faith with lurid contrasts of heaven and hell. We have become bound to rules and regulation. We have set up impersonal and intangible creeds. But that's not the faith that so many want—so many like Rikki Fulton, so many like me. Here is a gloriously universal faith. It is a faith of joyousness. It utters the most treasured promises of life today and new life tomorrow. And with a lot of love, we must start being shifted by this wind of God to tell of such things. It is a Pentecost love for the oppressed and a Pentecost prayer for a change of heart in the oppressor. It is a Pentecost love for the troubled in body and mind. It is a Pentecost love for the hungered. It is a Pentecost love for the war-weary and the war-wounded. And if all that sounds decidedly lacking in Church doctrines, I don't honestly care. If we can get hold of that sort of Spirit-filled love, we shall be real disciples out on mission with those who have gone before us.

And the third lesson is as important as the other two. If there is a universal wind of God, and if that wind is one which is dominated with love, then people today need to go outside and be swept along by its power. The wind in *Gone with the Wind* was one that swept across Tara and all its people in a tide they wished to staunch, but which swept them away. They tried to face into it and defy it, but they failed. But with Pentecost we have the wind of God with which we should run, rather than against which we should stand.

Pentecost swept the Apostles forward. It was the one event which made all the difference to their mission. One moment they had been given a word of resurrection to speak about, but they shuffled around Jerusalem, not terribly clear as to where or how to start. But filled with the Spirit they were made into men who were buoyed along to turn the world upside down for Christ.

Rikki wonders if the Church today is sufficiently upbeat—and so do I. I wonder if we are ready to be swept along. For isn't it true that all too often the wind of God is blowing and men and women are saying, 'Let someone else do it. I'm too busy. I'm too tired. I don't have the time. I'm shy. I don't think I could manage. I'm happy with things the way they are, even if they are downbeat, second-rate and patently failing'.

No. Come and stand outside. Stand in the wind where your excuses do not count any more. Stand where you cannot avoid the wind of God. Stand and let yourself be blown forward into Christ's world of mission. Stand and find that your own tongue can surprise you because you are able to speak about God and witness to God in a way you have not tried before. The wind of God is universal and you cannot avoid it. It is about love and therefore you cannot want to avoid it. It beckons you from behind your door and is a sound from heaven. It bids you to adventure. It fills the world. And it has nothing to do with old ghosts.

I wish someone had told me that a long time ago ....

6

Count me in?

ONE of the strange things that happens when you have an inquisitive member in your congregation is that, though you think you are trying to help him along in his search for truth and for God, he is stimulating that same search in you.

One summer day, I was having a thought-provoking chat with Rikki, when he said, 'Okay, tell me. Show me. Let me see. So many people have spoken to me about this thing called faith and it must be wonderful to have it ... but *how* do I know it's true?'

These questions are not new—he is asking what many, many people wonder. It's one thing to throw biblical texts at people, one thing to preach faith from the pulpit, but quite another thing really to tackle what is being said in the Bible and to look for new ideas, new thoughts, maybe something that has been staring you in the face but you haven't noticed before.

Later I sat in the study and read one of my favourite chapters in the New Testament—Paul's great hymn to love in 1 Corinthians (verse 13). Suddenly it was as if a sentence there jumped out at me, inspired by the day's talk. It was a line I had read many times before, and which had always brought with it a slight degree of anxiety. If I had suppressed that anxiety, it was Rikki who made me investigate what was maybe the beginning of an answer for him and just as much an answer for me—even if I had never thought of trying to find the answer before.

I found Paul's claims that 'now we see through a glass darkly, but then, face to face' (1 Corinthians 13:12) somewhat troubling. It is because of the contrast which Rikki had pointed out and which appears, at first reading, to be affirmed in these words. It is a contrast between the 'darkly' of faith as we seem to have to experience it now, and the 'face to face' which is only going to be offered after this life is over. But what Rikki says, and what I know to be true, is that it is in *this* life that we need help with religion—now when the things of God are stirring inside us and we want to know a bit more clearly what it's all about. Is Paul saying that it cannot happen? We must experience the 'darkly'? We cannot see? Is it bound to remain black, and must our faith merely grope about in the dark for the answers that in effect will have to wait until we have died?

Here many of us are on the search for faith. But is the search all in vain because there is nothing to find? No matter how hard we try—and there are some who try very hard—when you look into that glass, it is as near opaque as can be.

'Tell me about faith'—I can't tell you. 'Tell me about life and death and eternity'—and I don't know. 'Tell me about God in a world of upheaval where so often unkind and irrational forces look as though they are at work'—and I am as perplexed as you are. And I began to think about what Paul was saying here. Time after time it comes out the same, and there is a shudder inside me that the paradox of God is that you can go on and on hunting for him—but find only darkness. And then tomorrow, when people might be tempted to think that it's too late because we have had to deal with our three-score years and ten in the gloom of un-answered faith, only then will it all be laid out neatly for us, face to face.

People try with faith. They try time after time because there is something inside them that stirs whether they care to admit it or not. People search and they seek. But there is this infuriating barrier—when we look into that glass there is nothing but the taunting reflection of ourselves so that, when we look for help, there is none. You feel there has to be more, and so you go out looking for it. And then, when you get to this glass behind which Paul says God is to be found, and you look, the final irony is that you see only yourself. Beyond it is darkness and what stares you in the face is the image of yourself; so that if you want to be helped, all the glass does is to throw you back on yourself.

But that is hell. A whole school of thought describes that as hell. To admit that you are inadequate, to acknowledge that your life needs to be directed beyond yourself, but at the end of the day to be thrown back on yourself because there is nothing else. The only thing you are able to say to those expecting answers is, 'Wait'. But I don't see that it helps a man in the slightest to tell him that his search is valid and that there are answers, but that he will need to be supremely patient—even patient beyond the time of his death! And what is even more worrying is that this is how a lot of our teaching and preaching in the Church comes over to people, caricatured in that old phrase, 'Pie in the sky when you die'.

Maybe this is why 'I M Jolly' was born. There have been in our tradition so many gloomy, stern ministers whose conversation is about sin and separation, whose message has been one of how desperately hard it is for ordinary mortals to catch sight of God. Even if you think you have been touched by God, even if you think you have some sort of answer—your vocabulary still has to take note of the fact that it is hard and you have to persuade others that it is hard for them too. That is the way it is with God!

But I read that sentence of Paul's again. You know how it is when something is so familiar that you can't conceive of another angle to the phrase or word? And here with Paul's phrase the contrast is pretty stark—dark today and face to face tomorrow. But thanks to a chat with Rikki on this beautiful summer's day, my Bible was read with a finer toothcomb than usual—and what about the essential point in all of it, that Paul actually saw through the glass?

It is as easy as that. It stares you in the face when you finally notice it. Paul saw through the glass. Of all the meaning to be drawn out of this one verse from the Bible, the most obvious one can miss you time after time. Maybe other people don't have the same difficulty as I do. Perhaps the contrast had not struck them in the same way as it had struck me. But, then again, maybe I am not on my own and there might just be some others who have missed the point too. Paul says *through* the glass—he saw *through* it. I am sure that the things he saw now, in the present, were not all as lustred in the full glare of light as he might have wished, had he been spiritually greedy. Some of the things he saw were shadowed; some things were not able to be made out in clear focus; some things left questions to be answered no matter how hard Paul looked—and still the 'darkly' has its place. But, like a whole new meaning on the verse, even these things were seen. And they would go on being seen from now to eternity. Only now, whatever bits are seen darkly are then going to be seen face to face. And so you look in the glass and it's not a mirror, cruelly reflecting back your own image. You are crying out to be helped and to be shown—and you are not being offered merely a view of yourself. For you see through the glass darkly and what you begin to notice are the things of God. And when we understand it like that, a lot begins to slough off us.

So what sort of things can we view? Looking in the glass, it's not an Alice in Wonderland sort of fairytale that we can see. It is truth, reality. What did Paul see? What does *any* person see?

I believe, first of all, that what can be seen is the sheer wonder of the Creation of this world, together with the miracle of life enjoyed by people like us. I do not think that we have done a great service over the years to men and women in the Church by so much of our 'Jolly' teaching and preaching which has been patently world-denying. So many have been anxious to suggest that this world is no more than a cess-pit of sin and that our lives must inevitably be some sort of toilsome penance. The truth of it is that there are so many like Rikki Fulton who don't see it that way. And because the Church has appeared to be contradicting quite blatantly what these people feel in themselves about the world and about life, they have been turned off the Christian faith.

But the Bible doesn't see it that way. The eighth psalm of David is an example of uninhibited joy surging through the poet when he thinks of the world and the universe as being jewels of God's creative power. And it was the same with Jesus. So much of his teaching was grounded in the world which his Father had made—the lilies of the field, the sparrows of the air, the fish of the deep. Our Lord had an abiding love for the world and for people in the world, with a belief that he had been sent to redeem all of it. God thought we were worth it! Far from being a ghastly mistake which he must have regretted since the day he brought it all into being, it was worth every drop of Christ's blood to ensure that everything that was best in it could be brought back to wholeness.

And it is that wholeness which we shall see face to face. For the present, you have to admit of areas of darkness. You would be a fool to pretend otherwise. There are aspects about the rawness in our world and the animosities among people that make us look again and again at what it all means. And there are times I would concede when we are frustratingly distant from seeing as much as we would like to see. But, even if that is so, we dare not lay aside and forget the things that are there—the beauty of an ocean wave; the miracle of a springtime flower showing defiantly through the remnants of winter's snow. We look through the glass and these are the sorts of things we see. And sometimes we see it darker than we want; but then we shall see it all, face to face.

We also see Jesus Christ through that glass. Paul saw him. He saw the most wonderful life that has ever been lived. He saw grace and truth such as no man had ever set eyes on before. I would like to think that we see it too. There is a compelling fascination with Jesus Christ. We look in on the strange events that surrounded his birth. We see a young man influencing people by the power of love. We glance at a cross—normally the place for the execution of criminals, now a symbol that haunts the souls of people for the hope it offers. We gaze through the glass into an Easter Garden and we are more and more persuaded that something happened in that place which is probably the most significant single event in the whole of history. And again, when we look through the glass, we see dark things too. There are so many questions we would love to ask. There are colours we want to see clearer. There are ideas we need to have expanded. There is also the enigma of Jesus in the world today—even if tomorrow will be no enigma at all, for it will then be face to face. But still Jesus can be seen and he can be seen today.

It is also that way with many of the great forces in life. There is hope, for example. It's amazing how there is something inside all people that wants to keep hope alive. They say that as long as there's life, there's hope. It's true. In the best of circumstances and in the direst of circumstances, men and women cling onto hope. It's part of our life-force. It has to do with the tremendous will in people to perpetuate life. And even when we have to stare death in the face, we look through that glass and, somehow or other, we are able to detect a shadowed image of hope that keeps us going to the end, and beyond.

Similarly, there is love—that tie which binds people together as husband and wife, parent and child, friend and friend. Love is arguably the most important force of all that empowers us through life. Others have tried to subordinate its power at various times. They tried it in the camps of the Third Reich, in the gulags of the former Soviet Union, on the streets of Ireland, and in the tempestuous nations of the Middle East. Violent people have tried to destroy love so completely that others have looked in the glass to see if it has any future, or if there is any point in persisting with it.

They tried to eliminate love in Paul and mocked it with a sneering dismissal. And even when it was pretty dark, the same Paul was true to what he had said for so long: 'Now abide faith, hope, love, these three; but the greatest of these is love' (1 Corinthians 13:13). And if today we see it sometimes through a glass darkly, then tomorrow, for a fact, it will be face to face.

For me, and I hope for many others—that is an enormously liberating insight. It is to get away from the terrible contrast that comes from not quite seeing what the Bible is trying to tell us. It is really not the case that things are grimly hard to see now—so hard that you can only be thrown back on the hell of your own anxieties and weaknesses and decay. But it is the case that now, as well as then, we see through the glass. We see through it today. My task, along with so many others, is to try to help people to look at what their eyes can see, if only they are willing to look.

Such an approach can be positive and also encouraging—if I have any response to Rikki asking if he can *see* faith, then it can only be in this sort of way that I can respond. It is to try to put colour to what we see sometimes as dark; it is to have the persistence to do it; it is to admit that we might sometimes be frustrated, not by what we don't see, but by what we *do* see but cannot identify too clearly; it is to covet the excitement of what we see in the glass coming ever into sharper focus; it is to acknowledge that it can take a long time to happen, because faith doesn't always come to people out on the Damascus Road; it is to say that there is no *maybe,* but that today, if we look, we can see wonderful things when we look in the glass. And Christianity must embrace every level in the search.

We intend to go on looking together, Rikki and myself. For, as far as I'm concerned, he is counted in and not counted out. And we shall see things that the 'I M Jollys' of this world are perhaps too dull, too blind, too set in their ways even to notice.

7

Only is enough

Back from the General Assembly!

THE quadrangle in the forecourt of Edinburgh's New College is dominated by a large statue of John Knox. It represents Knox in what one would imagine to have been a familiar pose, hand outstretched while the bearded preacher is declaiming God's Word. Many years ago, entering the quadrangle, I was met by a young, fresh-faced, happy looking man who seemed to have slipped from the shadows of the base on which Knox stands. Without any introduction he launched his all-important question, not knowing who I was and not really caring either—'Are you saved?' Saved? From *what?* From *whom?*—until the significance sank in and I said, 'Yes, oh yes. I'm saved all right'.

His question was a religious one. It was to do with faith. He was anxious about the state of my soul. And he was so earnest about it all. Looking back on it, and still thinking about it, it is the sort of encounter that makes you feel just a little uneasy about your own approach to faith with its persistent questioning and its rather laconic style.

I told this story to Rikki on one particular visit, just after being in Edinburgh after the General Assembly, and it took us back again to what the Bible has to say about it. He too is conscious about that demeanour of some people in the Church which exudes certainty, yet at the same time succeeds in making you feel somewhat inferior for not being the same way. Many people

46

are like the man who fell off the edge of a cliff. It was a sheer drop of hundreds of feet to the bottom and, as he plummeted to his doom, he snatched out at a little shrub which was growing defiantly in the rock face. His fall was spectacularly arrested. But now he was swaying in no-man's land. It was impossible to get back to the top and all too easy to plunge to the foot. And so he shouted out, 'Is there anyone up there who can help?' Suddenly he heard a voice, saying, 'Yes. This is God. I can help you. But first of all, before I can do anything else, I have to ask you to trust me and let go of the shrub. Then I can help ....'

The man looked up and then he looked down again, and the enormity of the invitation became so great that he bleated out the appeal again, 'Is there anyone *else* up there who can help me?'

So much for faith and our own human condition. The man, after all, was only human—an expression which is part and parcel of vocabulary in whatever language you speak: 'I'm only this, only that, only human'. I'm not a great Christian, people say. I don't know as much as so many others. I don't have that shiny certainty that belongs to men who lurk in the shadows of John Knox. I myself might have wanted to check if there was any other means of help too! And because of this, there is the feeling that you cannot quite be as much in the Church as others—because you have not passed the test.

Rikki and I began our conversation from there and in the Bible found that there was once a young man who said exactly the same thing. 'I am only a youth,' said Jeremiah at the very moment he became aware of the extraordinary things God was asking him to do (Jeremiah 1:6).

So what about Jeremiah? He was a teenager, probably sixteen or seventeen years of age—it seemed as though God was asking the impossible of him. Where others had failed and where others would not have dared, Jeremiah was now being asked to go. God wanted him to go onto the streets and into the homes of men and women in Jerusalem and tell them about God and what God wanted of them. He had no training for this, other than the experience he had had of being what we would call 'a son of manse'. And, worse than that, the people were hostile to religion at that time. They belonged to a society that was in the process of disintegrating and which also faced severe problems of national security. The people didn't want to listen to anyone, nor did they have time to listen. Yet God spoke to Jeremiah, and said to him:

My friend, before you were born I knew you. I had a job in mind for you. And now is the time for you to do it. I want you to be a prophet to this nation.

~ adapted from Jeremiah 1:5 ~

Jeremiah said, as I think any right-minded teenager might say, 'But I'm only a youth!' And yet the strange thing is that, protestations done with, Jeremiah went on to become one of the greatest servants of the people and of God in the whole of history. And far from being a job for a cocky know-it-all, God chose a youth who 'was *only*' because *only* was enough.

And if Rikki and others are worried about being 'only', then there's a continuing weight of evidence to tell them that 'only' people are the ones who sometimes can be of greatest service in the cause of the Kingdom. Remember that it was another youth called David who slew the gigantic Goliath with a stone. It was only a child in a manger who represented the most staggering miracle the world has ever seen—God, mighty and eternal God, coming into the world in the flesh and blood of a mere baby. It was only a handful of basically ill-educated men who were asked to be the disciples of Christ. It was only a chance foreign visitor to Jerusalem who was there to carry our Saviour's cross. 'I am only' could have been the phrase on every one of their lips. Possibly it was. And if we want to look into the Bible to see if God can even begin to have a place for us today as 'only' people, then we ought to do so and find ourselves not discouraged by our failings, but encouraged by the way in which God thrives on the 'I am onlys'.

'It doesn't happen in other spheres,' Rikki reminded me. 'Apply for a job as a member of a theatre company and say *I am only me*—I cannot act, or speak clearly, or present an attractive personality—and you will be told not to call them, they will call you! Ask if you may play in a orchestra and tell the appointing committee that you love the sound of the violin so much that you went out and bought a Stradivarius which you cannot play, and I doubt you would get the job. And yet God's judgements about people don't work like that'.

That's right! God is not looking for best qualifications, best ability, best charisma, best prospects type of people—not that he would turn down these sorts automatically, because it's also true that some of the most gifted people in our society have also been some of God's best servants. But that is a coincidence and not a requirement. I think that is because God knows that the vast majority of men and women fall into the 'I am only' category. But *only* is enough with God's help, and it would amaze you what God can make of them.

I am *only* a teenager; I am *only* an old man; I am *only* a house-wife; I am *only* a new church member still trying to come to terms with so much in the Bible from the Amalekites to heaven itself! Don't go on saying things like that! It seems that it is part of our condition to decry ourselves, and maybe even to make it an excuse for standing on the sidelines of faith in fear that we aren't enough. We are so accustomed to being interviewed and audi-tioned and examined for other things, that we tend to think the same rules apply for faith. God tells us, 'No. You're wrong. It's not like that with me. *Only* is enough'.

God does not ask a young person to have a theology degree before he can be active for the Lord in prayer or service or witness. God doesn't recognise retirement ages in the Church because people cannot retire from faith. God doesn't want those who don't question or ask or probe into the thousand and one ways he is to be known, if only we have the courage to ask.

But the trouble is that we find it hard to believe God. We are so unadventurous at times. We have such a narrow and restricted view of what faith can be about. We forget that service to God can happen in so many ways, most of them probably quite small and almost certainly unseen by many. Believe God and believe that only is enough.

It can go further than that, however. What if you are struggling still with the faith itself. Unlike that happy man at New College, who knows he was saved at a time and a place he will be anxious to tell you about when he leaps from the shadows of Knox, I don't have it all button-holed yet. I can envy a man like that, but I'm not like that, and what about strugglers with the faith itself?

Fair enough! But if that's where you are today, then you find yourself in some pretty good company. Didn't Peter struggle with the faith? Or when he denied Jesus three times and ran in fear down the dark alleyways of Jerusalem's back streets, distancing himself as far as possible from the cross—was all that just a sham? Or when Thomas stood in the upper room and was told by his friends that they had seen the Risen Christ—didn't he struggle? Didn't he feel that he needed more than a word of faith? Wasn't it the nail prints he had to see and touch before he could accept it all? Didn't Martin Luther struggle with belief when he read the Bible day after day, night after night, and still it seemed to make no sense to him? Didn't John Wesley struggle when he felt a cold chill dampening his heart at the very times he was trying so hard to feel the warmth of faith? If you ask men and women to be honest, wouldn't they tell you that as Christians they have known what it is to struggle with faith, to be cast into a valley which is shadowed on every side? I don't believe people when they say that they *haven't* struggled with faith. Or at least, I believe that the faith they claim is a very colourless thing. I don't believe them if they say they have the whole of faith tied up. I don't believe this because the experience of so many of the *greatest of believers* is that they have known what the 'dark night of the soul' is, but have endured it to come out into a new morning, battered a bit, but so much richer.

And if anyone is struggling with faith at any time, today included, you don't have to be cast to the margins to feel guilty. I know it happens. People say, 'God can't use me because I'm not good enough. He can't use me because I don't believe firmly or constantly enough. He can't use me because I don't have that exceptional faith all the saints must have had'.

But perhaps the saints didn't have it either! Nonetheless God used Peter and Thomas and all the others—not because they were immune to struggle, but because they had been enriched by it. They had known times when they had been clinging to the last straw. And they too were wondering, 'Is there anyone *else* up there?'

All of these things belong to some of the most important attitudes I've tried to have towards people, wherever I've gone as a minister. I have tried to stand up for the 'I am *only*' people of faith: *only* young, *only* old, *only* a struggler, *only* ordinary. There's no other place it could happen. Top table Christians don't appeal too much. I'd much rather sit down at the far end among people I can talk to—and I'm pretty sure that many others like Rikki Fulton will be right there next to me!

8

I believe ...

Pre-holiday!

A FEW centuries ago, the poet Alexander Pope coined the phrase which has been used by many people in many circumstances—'fools rush in where angels fear to tread'. As time passed and discussion with Rikki began to home in on so many different and exciting questions of the Christian faith, the challenge was not always one way!

That particular day, when we were chatting, the conversation swung round to a new way of looking at things: not from unfaith towards faith, but from faith to *greater* faith. In reading the New Testament I came across again the well known story of the man who brought his sick son to Jesus to be healed. The disciples had tried to help but had failed, and the man now turned directly to Jesus. Almost with a hidden tone of frustration, Jesus tells the father that all things are possible to him who believes, to which comes the rather surprising reply, 'I believe, help my unbelief' (Mark 9:24).

I resolved to suggest to Rikki in answer to his self-doubt— 'Perhaps you believe much more than you *think* you do'. Here was a father whose son was probably an epileptic and whose condition caused a lot of worry to the family. It wasn't what the man had hoped for his son. Far from being a young person growing into the strength of youthful adulthood, this was a boy whose sickness was a debilitating thing. It wouldn't go away, and because of it the father was tested all the time. It was an illness that tested his patience, his endurance, his ingenuity and his faith.

'It's a bit like the way faith is tested in you,' I said to Rikki, 'how you struggle to find answers and become impatient with platitudes. You think it's such a struggle that it's hardly worth going on. You feel at the end of the line in terms of new ways of thinking and trying, and get to the point where the struggle of faith looks so hard that it's all pretty gloomy and hopeless'.

But when all that was said, and maybe acknowledged, we looked at what this man had said to Jesus. As the last cry, as the final statement, the man said to Jesus, 'I believe, help my unbelief'. And, all of a sudden, we were into new ground, looking at that sentence and at the order in which it was put.

The very first thing that the father says is that *he believes*. Inside him, whether he actually meant to say it or not, there is some basic, inherent, elemental belief. He probably couldn't put his finger on what it was; he maybe couldn't speak about it as coherently as a man of religion might speak about faith—but inside him, when it came to the final reckoning, he *believed*. And what he wanted Jesus to do more than anything else was to help him overcome what he did *not* believe. And that's a reversal, in fact, of so much of our searching.

The traditional way of coming to ideas of belief and unbelief, of probing with our questions in order to get some answers, is to assume that things are the other way round. It would suggest that a person ought more properly to be saying, 'Jesus, I *don't* believe. I really want to believe. I'm so anxious to have what I see other people having. But I don't believe. I have so many questions and so many problems with faith that I cannot come to grips with *any* of it. And yet there is this feeling inside that I need to know—that if I have a soul, then it is stirring with a desire to be satisfied. I do not believe. Help me to believe'.

And I talk to those in this situation and sense that this is the angle from which they are coming, because it is the angle which, I now think, the Church has been encouraging in people for far too long. It has been the assumption on which a lot of mission has been built. Here you have people who don't believe, and our job, through hell and high water, is to make sure that by the time we have done with them, they believe. That is why we have pulpit pleas for conversion from a life of darkness to a life of Christian enlightenment. It is what lies behind that specific sort of Christianity that asks a man or woman to hear God's word and, having heard, to come forward and be saved. There are thousands and thousands, we assume without even thinking about it, who do not believe, and it is by the persuasion of conversations and sermons that they will be brought from the intellectual darkness of unfaith to the intellectual light of faith.

Yet, dealing sensitively with a friend, I wonder if that is the whole story. I wonder even if it is the *main* story. And I wonder that because I'm not so sure that we are beginning at the correct point with them. That's why a fool might rush in where angels fear to tread. And let me be the fool.

Were men and women not born to believe? Whatever we make of the Creation Story in Genesis, there is an enormous wisdom to be found in the man who put the story together. In this great catalogue of all things that were made, mankind was both different and also special. Maybe we have lost sight of that. But mankind was made in God's image. He was, in the words of the Psalmist, created just a little lower than the angels and was crowned with glory and honour. He was made to be unique in the whole of Creation. He was created, not just as another animal, but to be God's partner in love. He had the singular ability to pray, to commune and to relate with God. Mankind was made to believe.

And that means that whatever our searchings and questionings,

54

and whatever wonderful conversations you can have about faith, we can begin from a starting point that few notice. The father who faced up to Jesus put the most natural feeling of all into words when he said that he believed. And yet it was just as natural too for him to ask Jesus to help him with the things he did *not* believe. For though we are made in the image of God, we are *not* God. We neither know nor do we appreciate the scope of his providence, and we have deeply clouded days when it is easy to lose our way in faith. But, nonetheless, when I, as a minister, speak to people in Church or anywhere else, then I ought to be able to begin with forgotten basics—that these are people who were born to believe. It is the most natural thing of all for people to do. And if we do not believe then we are, in some senses, denying our very humanity. And for me to say that to a friend starts us out at quite a new place.

But what about all the basic things we believe? We believe in a good world—at least I do and so does Rikki. We would be fools not to be impressed with the beauty of spring flowers, or the majesty of mighty waves crashing down on a craggy shoreline, or the birth of a child—or a thousand other signs that show the world to be filled with signs of miracles. People of Christian faith and people of no Christian faith, people of feeling and sensitivity, people of all varieties, believe that this world is a glorious achievement, however it was brought into being. Joseph Addison (1672–1719) wrote these great words in his hymn 'The Spacious Firmament on High':

In reason's ear they all rejoice, and utter forth a glorious voice,
For ever singing, as they shine, 'The hand that made us
* is divine ....'*

But I don't think Addison was overtly Christian. He was more

55

a *deist*—someone who has what I think is a rather limited view that there is a God, somewhere and somehow, but without being much clearer about it than that. But Addison believed in the miracle of the world and the miracle of life. And so do we. Lord, we believe.

But then the plea that follows in the second part of the appeal to Christ is just as important—'Help my unbelief'. Help me, in other words, to try to make some sense out of things when this wonderful world turns hostile. Help me when I see this world turning raw and bloody. Help my unbelief when I see famine, or terrorism, or when death claims someone out of time and season. Help me, said the father, when I see my son writhing with convulsions, because I don't understand as much as I want to.

Again, Rikki and I share a basic belief in life. He tells me that he gets the most enormous thrill out of being alive. I too love life. It is amazing that through all the maze of generations before us, what a miracle it is that everything fell into place to ensure that we are here now, alive and living. It is the most incredible thing. Yes, we love life. We believe in it—with all its potency and its opportunity and its friendships and its love. We love it for its challenge and its achievement. We love it and we believe in it and we do whatever we can to cling onto it, because it is a cup we do not wish to drain empty. And again the second part of the father's plea is important—help our unbelief.

Help us when life is threatened and death is stalking. Help us when we are being robbed of one of the greatest gifts that outmatches and outshines all others. Help us when we are deprived of someone with whom we have shared life. Help our unbelief then. Help my unbelief, said the father, when I see my son—the next generation—threatened by some wicked disease.

So far so good. But then what about this for an idea—that we are also born to believe in God. It is part of our being. It is the most natural thing in the world for a person to say, 'I believe in God', and the most unnatural to say the opposite. For we are also born with a soul. Unlike any other creature in the world, we are born with a soul and that soul is the direct link we have with God. Indeed, I would want to go so far as to say that to be an atheist is to deny one of the most basic parts of your own humanity. Wasn't there someone in the former Soviet Union who said that he never ceased to be amazed at how much effort Communists expended in trying to disprove what they believed didn't exist!

We believe. Something inside us, for lack of a better expression, pulls us towards God. And again it is right for us to recall the second part of the plea—help our unbelief. Who is God? Or what is God? Where can he, or does he, feature in our lives? What part does he play in our present or our future? When you son is convulsed, asked the man, when your son is shuddering with pain, help my unbelief in God.

So, there's the challenge from a different angle. It is natural to believe—to believe in our world, to believe in life, to believe in God. And as the man who met Jesus found himself able to speak of that sort of belief, so I am sure we can as well. And that's a far cry from the rather narrow and sometimes glib stereotype image of sheep and goats that pervades a lot of Church language. I don't want to be in a numbers game where I count conversions here and conversions there. I don't want to meet friends and scan pews wondering who is a believer and who is not. We don't need that oversimplified scenario any more, where you don't really listen to people because, if you do, you might have to change you own way of thinking about them and the things they ask.

I want to listen to the questions of those who search. I want to know all things that they believe already. I want to do that because questioners and seekers have some honest deep-down feelings and thoughts. They aren't shallow, uncaring, unthinking people who live a life of simple material pretence—as the unchurched in society are often condemned. It's far too easy to dismiss people like that and feel good about it. But the man who went to Jesus was not like that. And neither are people today. But what they ask me, and people like me, is what the man asked of Jesus Christ, 'Help my unbelief'. That's what men and women want now. So, let them recognise that they have a head-start already. It might be confusing at times. It might be that there are stubborn anxieties that are hard to deal with. They might even have some of their questions out of line with what they basically believe. But they need to be heard and they need to be helped.

Belief in the world—they want to see clearer how it is God's world. Belief in life—they want to see better how life conquers death. Belief in God—they want to have a relationship with God rather than a set of doctrines and dogmas about him. And that is what mission ought to be about. What I, as a minister, want to do is to turn these sorts of people and these sorts of questions more and more towards Jesus Christ. That is because experience itself, if nothing else, tells me that the more you turn to Jesus and the more you listen to his words and the more you try out his gifts of grace and love, the more unbelief will be swept away. Jesus did not minister among people who had no belief. They were filled with belief. But what they also had, people like the father who came to ask for help, were great areas of anxiety and doubt that impeded their faith. And as they came to him, so they found that these areas were eroded, bit by bit.

I'm not sure what the purists would say about it and I'm not too concerned anyhow. There must be so many ordinary people today with turbulent belief who are searching for their belief to be addressed. They have questions aplenty. They have huge grey areas about what they believe and how that sort of belief falls into place with everything else. And that recognised and, indeed, encouraged, I want to take courage in both hands and point unashamedly at the person, character, life and work of Jesus Christ. For I am quite persuaded that nothing else will help with unbelief. Nothing else will clear the clouded areas—everything else has been tried. Be glad about what you believe already. Talk about it. Then look to Jesus and find that, little by little, the unbelief will be stripped away. That's what *I* think certainly ... what about you?

9

What God thinks of Wimps

RIKKI said to me, soon after I got back from my holiday, 'You must get fed up with all these questions I ask you? Don't you find it easier when people just accept what you say and leave it at that?' He couldn't have been further from the mark. What minister worth his salt would be offended by opportunities for frank, honest discussion? I suppose you might be put off if you don't want to be made to think. Or if you feel you have all the answers so neatly tied up that no one should have the cheek to challenge you. Or if you want to pretend that you don't have time to waste on such conversations—what was that about the theatre padres having another appointment?

But I love it—and I do so because I think it's right and, more than that, because I think God loves it too. And it was from another little picture in the Old Testament that I set out to put Rikki's mind at rest.

There were two men called Esau and Jacob (Genesis 25ff). They were brothers. Esau, the elder by only a few minutes, was the apple of his father's eye. He was strong and daring, a hunter who faced life with a dashing, cavalier spirit. Esau was the sort of man who would have attracted attention for all the best reasons in any company and at any time. Jacob, however, was the younger twin, quiet and broody, the boy who sat around the house a lot and was fussed and pampered by Rebekah—a real mother's boy.

Jacob had time on his hands to think. And his thoughts became so calculating that they began to centre on trying to do down his brother. Was it jealousy that was eating away in the boy's heart?

Even as Jacob's father was dying, a time when a little extra respect might have been in order, the younger brother fooled Isaac into thinking that he was Esau and the dying man's blessing on the first-born was given to Jacob instead. It could not have been changed, for that's the way things happened then. And there's no point in saying that Isaac could have changed it when he found out he had been tricked, because custom dictated otherwise. Thus Jacob got what he didn't deserve.

'Now,' I said to Rikki, 'set these two boys in front of you and forget it happened all these years ago. Think of it as a family fight in which you, a reasonable man, might be able to come to some sort of conclusion. If you do like that, then you have to say, "Poor Esau—our hearts go out to you. And you, Jacob, confidence trickster par excellence, I don't like what you did and I don't admire it." Who could argue with you?'

Only God! God seems to have looked on it quite differently? Elsewhere in the Bible, in various places, God's verdict is summed up in these words, 'Jacob, I loved, but Esau I hated'. And the reaction that comes quickest to mind about this is it has to be unfair. We have to be ready to jump on people like Jacob. But God wasn't. So what about asking some questions about this, and let's see where the answers take us? If we do, it might be easier to understand why questions are so necessary.

In the first place, we cannot begin to doubt that God saw what was going on between the two brothers. If that is so, then we can assume that God is fair enough to have noticed what was good in Esau and devious in his brother. No one could say that Jacob was right to do what he did at that moment of his father's death, nor that Esau was wrong to feel indignant at being usurped by the combined wit of his brother and mother. So far so good, though I'm not sure Rikki knew quite yet where I was trying to take him! The silence and the furrowed brow were pretty good indicators!

Well, let's look at bit wider and try to see at least something of what God must have noticed in the two men that drove him to a different conclusion. Esau in fact, when you scratch deeper, was a man who did not care much about anything. Remember the time Jacob got the better of him for the sake of a plate of pottage —a thick vegetable soup! (Genesis 25:29) It really didn't matter much to Esau. He didn't see anything particularly important in it. And when this deathbed blessing was given to his brother, of course Esau was cross. But it wasn't a burning sort of anger that would do anything to retrieve its loss. Esau was like a lot of people —he was a huffer and puffer. His mother knew it and so she counselled Jacob simply to go away for a while till it all cooled down—and that's exactly what happened! What God saw in Esau went a lot deeper than what you and I notice at first sight. Like us, God could see that Esau was strong and good and attractive in many ways; but what we don't see right away was that Esau was also as bland as milksop, pliable, so little committed to anything at all that there was nothing in fact worth troubling his life for.

In a similar way, God saw deeper down into Jacob than we do. Certainly he was a rogue, and sometimes people would get the better of him just as he had got the better of his brother. And there's little arguing that people like Jacob need to be pulled up from time to time. But God saw further than that. He saw Jacob as a man of imagination. There were times the imagination got him into trouble. But what potential there was in that imagi-nation at its best. What potential there was in a man who could sleep rough in the night and dream of angels on a ladder between earth and heaven. Esau would have ridiculed a dream like that. He would have asked no questions—because Esau was a spiritual wimp! Yet Jacob was moved by the dream and, in order to remember that it happened, and to remember *where* it happened, he set up a small altar. It was a marker post at Bethel and it has been a marker post to God ever since.

And so it continued with Jacob until the day came when his curiosity and questions came to a head in a remarkable encounter with God. The Bible talks of it as a time when he wrestled with God—he wrestled and struggled in the night with his questions. He wouldn't give in, wouldn't yield until God had given him a blessing. And could that be the blessing of an answer? This was no wimp then. This was not a man who didn't care one way or the other. And in the end, with the struggle over and the blessing finally achieved, Jacob left the place of struggle at Peniel with the sun on his back—and with a limp to show what a great struggle the whole thing had been. 'Jacob, I loved, but Esau I hated,' said God. And I can just about begin to see why.

And so we come back to Rikki's persistent questions. Take the Church of these times. I think that it is so often far too similar to Esau. At a superficial level there's so much about it which is strongly cavalier. It goes out on the hunt at times and doesn't much mind who it knocks over and who it offends, if it senses a righteous indignation. It's good at taking up causes and shouting about them from the rooftops. Or again, it can be neat and ordered with a prim, prissy life that is simply waiting to pounce on the sinner and squash him. It possesses God's blessing and no one can ask difficult things of it, no one can challenge it, no one can take its birthright away from it. It knows its pecking orders and who is at the top of the tree and who is at the bottom.

But what does it do for its people? It doesn't have time. It appears to resent being questioned. It is too busy to expand its agenda, even if you have questions for that agenda that are deeply serious and affect the final destiny of your soul. Too bad! I've got another engagement. Perhaps we should get the diary out and arrange another time. And I doubt very much if we are, as a Church, as fully aware of the frontier land where we live today as we ought to be. People's souls are at stake. And I find myself asking more than ever if we are as a Church spiritually, manly enough to do our job. Does God detect in us more of the reliable, stolid Esau than the provocative Jacob.

I'm sure God longs for a Church with imagination. He yearns for a Church that wrestles and struggles. Yes, it might make mistakes and not do a very good job of covering its tracks when it does. It might need to take a few risks to get God's blessing. It may well find itself dreaming the oddest dreams and setting up the most unlikely altars where it has seen these dreams. But I'm in no doubt at all—God wants to see a Church that genuinely wrestles with him and tries to work out what he means as we move towards the twenty-first century. Only that sort of Church is manly enough for the task. People *are* hunting for faith. They *are* looking for answers. They *are* as anxious now to see God's face and know God's love and sense God's hope as men and women have ever been. And they are in our society and in our world in their droves.

But they won't find what they're looking for in a Church which is wimpish. They won't find it in a Church which, like Esau, puts up a good front, knows the rights words and jargon, but has no stuffing to it. God looks to see a Church that is wrestling— so hard perhaps that some of the jargon and some of the prejudices will become dislocated and we shall for a time walk with a limp. But, just as surely, the sun will rise on that sort of Church and it will be the real successor to Jacob, who God so fervently loved. And when you are asking questions, I say to Rikki, it's not to do with time or anything else like that. Your questions ask of me the honesty not just to hide behind the Church, but to come out openly and wonder if I myself am to be cast in the mould of Esau or Jacob.

Why did I become a minister of the Church? What does the faith mean to me, that I want to talk about it and communicate it? Why am I involved? What am I trying to do and to see for today and tomorrow? And is there any danger at all that I find the comfort of slipping into the pattern of Esau far more appealing than being out where people ask awkward questions. It's very easy to fall into the trap of thinking that Church membership is simply belonging to a club of nice people. That's not altogether untrue. I suppose I have found Church people to be, by and large, a warm and friendly lot. I like the organisations and the friendships and what would be called in churchspeak, the 'fellowship' of it all. It's not *all* wrong. But if that's all the Church means to me, and all that I ever want it to mean, then my name is Esau and I'm not so sure that God would be any more thrilled at me than he was with Esau all these centuries ago.

God wants people of imagination. He wants people with enough nerve to dream—and having dreamed, to have enough wit and imagination to try to put these dreams into effect. He wants people to wrestle with him. There are far too many who simply soak faith in as if they were a sponge, who accept things so easily that when the day comes when it is put to the test, they find out that it can be shed just as easily. God loves people to wrestle with him. As a minister, I like it as well, for so much of that spiritual wrestling is done during thought-provoking conversations which, in themselves, are so stimulating. What does it mean when you say that God has a purpose for you in life? Have you ever wrestled with what death means for you, and with what eternity might mean? Have you really wrestled with things like that? Every time that we do, God sees us; and even though we might end up with the mark of spiritual battle so seared into us that we are going to walk with a limp for a time, God loves it.

'I never get fed up with your questions,' I tell Rikki. 'Only wimps in life and wimps in soul don't wrestle and ask and keep on trying—and they are the successors to Esau whom God so hated for being like that. You're like Jacob—and I think that's great! And so, by the way, does God'.

10

Fossilised Faith

S OME ministers tell me that they like 'Last Call' with the Revd I M Jolly—but they do so through gritted teeth! I suppose that you only have to look at some correspondence in official Church publications to see that there is a section in the Church which views this masterclass satire with less than full approval. And so I had a word with Rikki to try to find out why.

It was about the same time that I had been having another quick look at some parts of that classic of English literature, *Great Expectations* by Charles Dickens. I was talking to Rikki about Miss Haversham who was stood up on her wedding day. All the arrangements had been made—but there was no bridegroom and, therefore, no wedding. Later in the book Dickens gives us another picture of Miss Haversham and her surroundings. She is wearing the same wedding dress, but now it is shaggy and grey having picked up the dust of the passing years. The wedding cake is also there, but it is mouldy and done. Miss Haversham is quite simply stuck in time, locked into yesterday, so that the years have passed her by and she has never quite come to terms with what happened to her.

Before we comment on how ridiculous she was, I wondered if we ought not to care. If we look at her and her situation, then we might just begin to understand why it is that churchmen sometimes grit their teeth when 'I M Jolly' is mentioned. And beyond that, we notice too that it was a similar issue with which our Lord Jesus Christ had himself to deal. In the great resource book of the Bible, it was a reaction that was met head on in the New Testament.

Rikki and I thought for a time about Jesus and how he spoke in these terms, 'You have heard it said .... ' He came out with the catalogue of what people of his day had heard said about religion. But Jesus knew that they were locked in the past. The laws were etched on tables of stone, and whatever these laws said had to be followed syllable by syllable. Any other way of thinking or reasoning or understanding was simply blinkered out. The law said, for example, 'You shall not kill'. It was clear as that—and, with the Jews' own particular brand of legalism, they were convinced that they were keeping it.

But then Jesus injected something new. His implication was that their attitude was not enough. There had to be more than a smug self-satisfaction that you are doing things only by the letter of the law. The law was not just about the physical slaying of a person. Rather it embraced attitudes concerning the dignity of men and women. It was about a person's total relationship with another. And anyway, for most decent-minded souls, the law about not killing someone was self-evident and pretty easy to keep.

Jesus took them that radical step further—beyond the fossilised traditions with which they had become so disastrously comfortable. He told them that they had to bring their anger with other people into the reckoning. They had to consider the insults they could throw at others because they too were connected with offences against our fellow men and women. And, one by one, he took their treasured preconceived laws and ripped them apart.

You have heard it said that adultery is sinful, Jesus told them—but I say to you that *lust* is just as sinful. You have heard it said that you should love your neighbour—but I am telling you that you should love your enemies as well.

One by one he took their traditions and led them beyond that until they found themselves in unchartered territory. But the people were stuck. Like Miss Haversham, they were dowdy and grey and living in the past. Their minds and souls were dull because they had ceased thinking about what God had really been trying to say to them. And all the while, they were protected and encouraged into thinking like this by the priests who had so neatly arranged things for their own benefit that they could do nothing other than resist and suppress new thought.

Of course, it has often happened like that. Even before Jesus there was a rebellious, offbeat preacher called Amos who found himself speaking about religion to men and women who were locked into their own little world of intrigue and comfort and compromise. And the preacher prophet told them that they couldn't go on like that. They couldn't allow the cobwebs to ensnare them. Fat, sleek people you are, exploiting the poor. Hypocritical worshippers, loving to be seen and flaunting skin-deep faith in the face of others. It was torrid stuff—far more satirical at times than I M Jolly has ever been! And years after Jesus, there were those bold enough to tackle the same issues. Martin Luther said it to a Church that had grown corrupt and tired. John Wesley said it to a Church which had become cold and calculating. But whenever people have said it, or forced us to examine it, there are going to be some who don't like what they see because it's altogether too close to home.

Amos was despised by the establishment. Jesus was hunted down by pharisees and saducees until they cornered him at Calvary, thinking they had managed to do away with him. Luther was ex-communicated. Wesley was branded as a disturber of the cosy establishment. And so we have to recognise that even to raise the subject, to make people think about their traditions, is to raise the temperature of faith. But we have to do it if we are not, like Miss Haversham, going to wallow in the past where faith becomes a museum piece and our own life with God a lie. The Revd I M Jolly is a mirror for every Christian to look at and, having looked, I shall risk being just as provocative and I want to be, if I think it is for the good cause of Christ and his Kingdom.

Together with anyone who is concerned for the Church, we can look at areas of our spiritual life that are with us now. And so let's start with some of the practicalities of religion. Perhaps there is a lot of it which sounds a bit too comfortable? Tripping off the tongue we can hear phrases like, 'God is a God of love'. Or 'God is a forgiving God'. We listen to many people nowadays telling us that if you live a good life or a moral life, it doesn't honestly matter what name you give to God—because we are all heading in the same direction anyhow.

How about the phrase, 'Jesus is not necessarily unique'? He may not even be crucially important in issues of life and death. Well, all I have to say is that such views, often encouraged by so-called Christian writers and teachers, have dragged Christianity into a sleepy lethargy where we loosen our grip on what we believe uniquely to be true of Jesus Christ. 'But I say to you,' said Jesus, 'I say to you, "I am the Way, the Truth and the Life." I say to you, "No one comes to the Father but by me"'. If that is so, then perhaps we should be a lot clearer in setting before people the above claim of Jesus Christ. The suggestion is that if, having heard of him, the people choose to reject him, then we believe that of their own free will they are choosing to reject him for their life and for their future and for their eternal destiny. That sounds like the stuff of good hell-fire.

But I believe that some things, perhaps unpopular, have to be said. Of course, there are those searching for God. Don't I know it! But they are quite a different issue. I'm talking here about wishy-washy faith where neither a search nor a sense of commitment matter. Too often the Church remains politely quiet, when instead it should be saying: 'I don't believe you. I don't believe your weak excuses and your sweet reasonableness. I don't believe your protestations of faith when your God is so vague and general as to mean nothing and demand nothing. I don't believe you find God on the golf course on a Sunday morning. I don't believe that you pray to God when you're pruning your rose bushes. I don't believe that you are committed to God as you tramp through the hills on a weekend'.

I believe we have to make these points and tell whoever will listen that, as many have done in their struggle for a real faith, they too can come a good deal nearer to God in the fellowship of worship than anywhere else. But I don't for a moment think that this is a universally popular thing to say, because it shakes suppositions that many socially comfortable Christians enjoy having.

Or again, you can be even more basic than that. You can enjoy the satire of the Revd I M Jolly as much as you like, but satire hurts when, deep inside you, you know that it's pointing to something that has a grain of truth to it—even more than just a grain. Jolly could be striking a few raw nerves in the very life of the Church. Why is it that within Church communities, more than almost anywhere else, deep hostilities and divisions can be found? How is it that tongues which can pray together the words of the Lord's Prayer can just as quickly become tongues that incite malice and gossip? Why is it that Church people often feel the need to get their own way in things? What makes Churches develop internal groups and factions?

It may be easy to dismiss questions like these as trivial and say that things have always been like that. But surely Jesus Christ is saying something quite different to us! Through the Apostle Paul, Church people are being told:

Love is patient and kind. Love is not jealous or boastful. It is not arrogant or rude. Love does not insist on its own way. It is not irritable or resentful. It does not rejoice at the wrong but rejoices in the right. Love bears all things, believes all things, hopes all things, endures all things.

~ 1 Corinthians 13:4-7 ~

And certainly what the Bible tells us is not always meant to be comfortable, if, by comfort, you mean weak and compromising and second-rate.

Perhaps the Revd I M Jolly attacks the cliches and assumptions and old-hat opinions that still hold back our Church from its vigorous mission. It's not meant to—it's not an attack on the Church—indeed that's the last thing Rikki would want it to do. But the very fact that it is sometimes spoken of through gritted teeth points to its ability to make some people feel that the cap is fitting rather too tightly for comfort. And if we are content to stay unchanged; if we resent anyone pointing these sorts of things out to us, in whatever manner; if we are so dull as to believe that we have all the answers already and can learn nothing new—then Miss Haversham is alive and she bears our own name now.

On the other hand, if we listen to Jesus and allow ourselves to be open to a scrutiny of mind and soul, then what a difference could be made in us, in our Church and in our society. 'But I say to you … ' is the constant and sometimes unnerving challenge. And if we are bold enough to face up to it, it can be the start of discovering a new set of blessings. People who are hunting for faith and for Christ will not find them in clichés. They will not be satisfied by little people with little answers. The road we take is far more exciting than that.

To share another person's exploration of faith is the very adventure of which our Bible so openly talks. We are not in the business of dead tradition and 'Jolly' clichés. We are here to excite vision and dreams and so to work our way towards the truth. Big issues lie deep in the souls of ordinary people. They want to know of life and death, joys and sorrows, and how religion is going to help them handle these sorts of things. Miss Haversham is quite useless for that sort of task. People who are locked into yesterday with a fossilised faith have nothing to offer. Pharisees and saduccees gritted their teeth when the cavalier young Christ satirised the poverty of their religion. They were unequal to the needs of their hearers.

So, what then is the Revd I M Jolly saying to us today?

11

Amalekites and the Rest

ONE of the big breakthroughs on our common hunt for faith began with a talk Rikki had with me about the Amalekites (1 Samuel 15)! I know I've still not answered their plight as fully as I should, and until I do I'm sure the question will keep coming back. But there was a beginning at least!

Rikki's concern, and the concern of many, rests in the claim that the Bible is God's Word. It is a claim which, to the logical mind searching for faith, implies that God is the author of the all words, incidents, attitudes and actions of everything that happened in the turbulent millennia that separated the dimmest early days of Genesis from the complex final words of John in the Revelation. The Word of God is exactly that. God said slay the Amalekites— and it was done. It was as simple as that. But it does raise the question as to why God would do that? Why should God say that seemingly innocent people should be slain, cut in pieces, destroyed? And if that is the sort of God he is, and if the Bible is the sort of book it appears to be—God's Word—then from a position of enquiry about the Christian faith there are people who are going to wonder if they want to get tied up with a faith as violent as that.

It is true that if you read the Bible then you discover that the Holy Land was not always holy. It was, at times, a hard and hostile place. It possessed an environment in which people could as easily suffer from life as they could benefit from it. It was a place of wolves and wars and woes. It was a land where weeping could be heard in town and country as often as the joyous sounds of people. And it was a place which gave testimony to human cruelty and indifference, amongst which is the final plight of the Amalekites. We can call it the Holy Land, but we have to recognise at the same time that unholiness scarred its surface and its years as well. The Holy Land harboured as many forces of evil and destruction as any other land. And part of the basic search for faith must, at some stage, deal with the reality of ordinary life, indeed the events of that ordinary life are called 'the Word of God'.

Here was a serious sticking point. As a Christian, you tell someone that God's Word is a wonderful word of grace and truth and love. But the searcher in Church listens to you reading what you call the 'Word of God', the God he or she wants to discover, and you are speaking verses that tell of Agag being hewn in pieces and God commanding his people to go and slay a tribe, their men and women and children, and to make sure that not a single one of them is left alive. You can see the problem!

At least it's a problem if you have the honesty to face the question. I suppose you can simply say that that's the way God's Word is and you have to accept it—a deadhand, traditional sort of approach for some. Indeed, I remember a biblical fundamentalist some years ago telling me that God had put stories like these in the Bible to fool people like me who ask too many questions! I'm not so sure that the searcher for faith would find much sympathy in that sort of approach.

But the fact remains that the Bible is uniquely the place for Christians in which God's Word shines through. In all the reality of life, with its great catalogue of human experience, it is in the Bible that God addresses men and women; and where they, in their turn, try to address themselves to what he is saying to them.

You can talk about the Word being 'contained' in the Bible, though again there are purists who would reject this sort of 'containerism'. You can talk about the sheer humanity of the biblical authors, though that does scant justice to the activity of the Holy Spirit in the lives of those who were writing. But whatever you do, the common search with the enquirer after faith, demands that we find some common ground where God's Word in the Bible makes sense and is consistent with everything we like to say about his nature of unremitting love and hope.

What the people of biblical times did was to remember the high times, the significant occasions when their lives were touched spiritually by God. They knew that a lot went on that was ordinary, but they also knew that here and there a picture was being pieced together that pointed ever more conclusively to the fact of God in the world, God in their history, God as an involved, loving person in their midst. And they set up cairns and they planted trees. They built sanctuaries. They were unafraid to say that here and there along the rocky road, God had met them and that the meeting had made a real difference. They were not shy about religion. They were keen to demonstrate just how much God meant to them, and so they planted trees, as it were.

Abraham planted a tree. At a moment when God's presence had brought him and Abimelech a peace that bound them in a covenant they knew they couldn't have fashioned without him, Abraham planted a tree. It was a tamarisk tree intended as a sign and a memorial. It was a tree to which he could keep on going back, because it would remind him in this often unholy land that this at least had been a place where, for a moment, he had walked on holy ground. And if ever the fact of God was becoming a touch dim for him, Beersheba's tamarisk tree would remain a shrine to remind him of the other side of things. That's the way it was. It was that sort of attitude which spawned the Bible. Men and women were open to look for God and to see God. That's why, in the end, Israel became a fit place to welcome God's own son. The places multiplied because the experiences multiplied—Beersheba, Bethel, Gilgal, the Temple set high on a hill they called Zion. Place after place and time after time, the unholiness of ordinary life was crossed with the holiness of God; and priests and prophets and poets wrote about all of this, holy *and* unholy, in what we now call the Old Testament of our Bible. Because of the shrines and the trees, people were recalled to things that had once been true for them and still were, even if they sometimes forgot it. Even when they suffered a huge military defeat and were taken, as a people, into exile, they discovered that the trees planted through their past still had a capacity to quicken the soul.

How shall we sing the Lord's song in a foreign land? If I forget you, O Jerusalem, let my right hand wither. Let my tongue cleave to the roof of my mouth, if I do not remember you, if I do not set Jerusalem above my highest joy.

~ Psalm 137:4-6 ~

That's the way God lived and that's the way the Bible came to be fashioned; and whatever we try to call it, that's the way we have to look at our Bible and read our Bible and share with the searchers like Rikki Fulton, the truth in the Bible. It was the means by which souls were fed—no more so than when another tree was planted on a hill called Calvary. Maybe it was because planting trees had been much more than gestures: it had been part and parcel of the foundation of faith that the sheer symbolism of the tree on Calvary had such an electric and immediate effect on people.

Maybe we should look at our faith today in the same way. Maybe we need to take time when we are, in effect, still planting these trees. The people who wrote the Bible remembered the precious times. They marked the place and the time when God addressed them. And I have to wonder if today we allow the times to pass us by, and we forget the places because we don't have the eye that is practised in looking for God. The world could do with more trees being planted now. We could all do with taking time to remember precious conversation, a high-lighted moment of worship, the occasion where we knew that God had been present, even if we hadn't put it in as many words. All of us have to do that—for God goes on speaking his word today, even in all the unholiness of so much around us.

And if we once called the poor unfortunates the Amalekites, they are identifiable today by other names. Unholiness and pain still stalk where we might rather see holiness and serenity. Ravaging events still produce their own sense of forsakenness. Men and women still look to see God. But where once there was Beersheba or Bethel or Calvary or an Easter Garden, today it seems to be a lot harder to see the shrines that we have planted in order to remember. Yesterday's trees have not been sufficiently tended to help us any more.

The old tree of Calvary is still there after all. It was the late Lord George MacLeod of Fuinary who said that Jesus was not crucified in a cathedral between two candles, but on a cross between two thieves. We need to recall ourselves to that. Maybe people today sometimes wish that God could understand how sore and perplexed they feel, how broken they sometimes can be. But he does know. And there is a tree at Calvary to tell us still that he knows. It is a tree that tells us that love is stronger than hate, and life is infinitely more conclusive than death. In the days of trouble it is a marker still to be found, for God was there and God knows.

There are other 'trees' too. Obviously they are not literally there, like the tamarisk, but they are constant reference points to areas in our lives where God has shown himself and where we have known that to be so. There is the power of a prayer, with the weight of incalculable achievement that has been won through prayer over the years. There is the fact of love and the incontestable evidence that it remains, as it has always been, the most potent of forces in our world. There is the special moment of what could be called providence when, though you may not identify it at the time, nonetheless you know in retrospect that an unseen hand has had something to do with guiding you along the right way, which otherwise you would not have found. There is the occasional moment in worship when, together with others who are with you, you experience a feeling for God, an awareness of God, which just for that moment seems to go beyond faith and become knowledge itself.

In the Bible these sorts of things would have been high moments. People would have talked about them and set up cairns or established sanctuaries or planted trees. These moments would have happened in the middle of a whole lot of other events—the slaying of the Amalekites included—which have to be addressed, but which do not diminish or obliterate the fact of God in our world. And that openness to God which helped create the Old and New Testaments, which lay behind a variety of authors genuinely telling us of God's word in our world, and which, as a result, lay behind the writing of the Bible, is an openness that is much needed today. The world needs more 'trees' to be planted. It needs more trees like Israel's which went on and on adding to the marker places which dressed the unholy in the garb of God.

The waters of the Red Sea were ordinary and remain ordinary. One day they were parted for the people of God and became the holy ground of the Passover. There was what looked like a pile of stones, to ordinary eyes, set high on the hill called Zion—and indeed they were no more than ordinary stones. But to the visitor in faith they were holy stones, where he could walk in the spiritual footsteps of his fathers and kneel at an altar where, even if for a short time, heaven and earth seemed to be one and the same thing. There was a Mount where the greatest sermon ever preached was delivered to men and women hungry for truth. There were ordinary village squares in Galilee where Christ taught and healed. There were quiet places where he prayed and evening conversations with John which were to create a Gospel that men and women would love for evermore.

And today, if we can unscramble for people like Rikki Fulton the confusion of the Bible, if we can address properly the questions of godlessness and cruelty in what is claimed to be the Word of God, if we can begin to show that the paradoxes are only apparent and not real—then we shall not only have gone a long way in helping people find faith, we shall also have gone a long way in helping people plant their own trees and talk about their own faith. The fruits are there. People will listen if we talk to them person to person about the Amalekites and the rest.

12

Christmas again

IN the hectic days when he was still in pantomime, Rikki never failed to make haste from the Christmas Eve performance to be at the Midnight Service in Church. For so many people, myself included, it is one of the very special services in the year. The challenge for a minister is to try to ensure that what is special about it rises above the emotion and the *bonhomie* which are themselves in abundance that night. What does Christmas really mean and offer? Without suppressing the happiness of the service, what can be done to give people a sense of the joy that belongs, not to Santa Claus, but to the birth of a Saviour who is Christ the Lord?

I told Rikki a funny story once, a story my own father told me years ago from his own experience as a teacher. It was near Christmas time and, as classes often do at that time of the year, various projects were being done relating to Christmas. My father was headmaster and went to visit a primary class. He gave them an art project—'Read some part of the Christmas Story from the Bible,' he told them, 'and then, using your imagination, draw a picture connected with what you've read'.

At the end of the period he went round the room looking at the various offerings. One young boy had drawn a great picture of a donkey, with Mary sitting on its back holding an infant, and Joseph walking alongside. But behind them all was a black dot or smudge which, my father remarked, appeared to remove some of the effect of the drawing.

It was an unfortunate smudge. A stain—a great pity. But the boy said that it was neither a smudge or a stain—it was in the Bible.

'Well, show me what you mean,' was the immediate response.

The boy pointed to the Bible, still open on his desk, and to Matthew chapter 2, at verse 13: 'Take the child and his mother and *flee* to Egypt ....' Yes, you guessed it—the black dot was the flea! It was wonderfully naïve, a classic of its kind—but I believe that it indicates a bit of the naïveté of Christmas that belongs not just to children, but to all of us.

If you are helping men and women search for the truths of the Christian faith, then the time when God's Son was made flesh and born in a stable in Bethlehem is surely one of the most critical moments of all. You can sing the carols and read the familiar lessons. You can sound happy and cheerful. But if people think you are talking about a fairy story, they will put up with what you say for a day and quite properly forget it and you tomorrow. That's what they did in the Bible, after all. Jesus was born. He was made flesh. But when he came to his own home, his own people did not receive him. These words are read at countless Christmas services and I wonder if people realise just how staggering they are and how contemporary!

Jesus came. He was born in the miracle of Bethlehem, he was raised in Nazareth, he was raised to know the faith of his fathers, he was ready to do God's will, he was prepared to offer forgiveness and life and hope and, in the end, eternity—but when he came with all that promise to his own people, they would not receive him or what he had to say. There was the day he stood in the Synagogue and started preaching. We might imagine that they would have been proud of the local boy, a lad o' pairts—but they were not. Instead Jesus was faced with a sneering snobbery—the carpenter's boy should know his place. Again when he healed ten lepers, nine of them did not even bother to say thanks. And despite the fact they cheered his triumphant entry into Jerusalem, within a week they were baying for his blood. Even Peter, in whom Jesus had invested such time and love, ran off, saying that he didn't know him.

It's not just the primary schoolboy who misread what Jesus was about. It was a whole crowd of adults in his own time. And the way we sometimes talk about Christmas and react to Christmas —that same crowd of adults is still with us. In Christ's time the people thought that they needed and wanted a warrior. They were held down by the Roman Empire and they believed that God would enter the stage with the might of arms; and with a Messiah they would wipe the earth clean of the invader. The Christ was to ride the world at the head of a heavenly army and the sooner it happened the better. But they did not want the sort of Christ they saw in Jesus and so they did not receive him. And we have to ask what sort of Jesus Christ we want today. What do we want from the man? What do we expect from the celebration?

First of all, let me make it quite clear that nothing should take away from the happiness of the event. I've said enough about long faces and I've distanced myself as far as possible, I hope, from Mr I M Jolly to show that the mournful front of what passes in some as Christianity is repellent to me. But it doesn't stop me wondering what people want from Christmas. Do they want it to be altogether different from the rest of the year? Are we so laid back at Christmas that it ceases to be a time when we face up to the questions and go out on the hunt as we have tried to do for the rest of the year? Is it time off? Is it to be a vacation from challenge, when we wrap ourselves up in colourful traditions and enjoy the coziness of carol singing with mince pies? I have to say that this feeling appears to prevail. Let us sing the carols again, retell the favourite Bible stories, deck the hall, light the lights and share out the presents. But let us leave it at that, because it only happens once a year and things are grim enough the rest of the time without making us think too much at Christmas as well. Let us call a smudge a flea—for who cares anyway?

Rikki asked me what ministers felt about the unfamiliar faces in church at the Watchnight Service, those who are not there the rest of the year. But isn't that the reason? Isn't that why our pews are filled with new faces at Christmas Eve? Isn't that why we welcome the baby with joy and thanksgiving and praise? They find it an escape. Next week they will not be there, because they do not want to receive the Christ for what he is. A baby is harmless and always creates feeling of well-being. Babies cannot talk. They cannot challenge. They do not call for discipleship. They never demand spiritual commitment. Babies don't get crucified. And so we can feel good about the baby in Bethlehem, but run from the man in Jerusalem—even from the boy in Nazareth, come to that.

In order to justify this—as they justified it in Christ's own time—people offer excuses, that become their reasons, for not receiving him. They say that things are not as happy in church for the rest of the year. The hymns aren't so good. The ministers are boring. There's someone to meet on the first tee at 11 o' clock. There's the lawn to cut, the car to wash, the paper to read. It's the only day they have to do the housework. In Jesus' time what they wanted was a conquering warlord—what they want now is an occasional merry Santa Claus.

But when people still rush from their work to be in church for a Christmas Eve Service, and when there are still countless people who want or need to hear something of the wonderful good news of our Lord, it is sheer dereliction of faith to pander to the excuses. I hope I never talk of fairy stories when I talk of Jesus. I trust that the sense of expectation and celebration is as evident for the rest of the year as it might be at Christmas. I am persuaded that the greatest word of Christmas is the word 'love', and that that word is as appropriate in June as it is in December. God so loved the world that he gave his only begotten son that whoever believes in him should not perish but have everlasting life. 'Love came down at Christmas'—but love came to grow and to challenge in a manner that can change the very direction of our lives. Someone once suggested that there is nothing terribly remarkable about love at first sight. It is when people have been looking at each other for years that love becomes remarkable. And if I talk to anyone, friends or otherwise, about God's love then it is only effective if it is for years.

Another great word at Christmas is 'peace'. It is said that if you look back into history, then about the only time when the whole world stood unburdened of the misery of warfare was the time Jesus was born. Now that may or may not be true, but if it is, then what a great symbol it offers us. Jesus and Christmas are certainly to do with peace. But then again, do people honestly want peace? 'Peace on earth and mercy mild'—we sing it lustily. Of course we are happy to hear of peace in our world at any time. But peace doesn't begin and end there. Do we honestly want to have the awesome power of peace in our lives? It can shake us. There are times when we feel a bit uneasy. We wonder about our life and its direction and purpose. After all, our lives are once-and-for-all things. We only get one chance and, if you're like me, then occasionally you might wonder about our values and ambitions. We ask ourselves about the things we find important or not important. And I have to say that if we ask these sorts of things while remembering our faith in Christ, the answers are not always as easy as we would like them to be. We can claim peace and goodwill on the Christmas cards we sign, but it's a more comfortable thing to leave it at that—a passing cliché on a greeting that is taken down on Twelfth Night. To make peace our own, in our own lives, means that we are asked to make Jesus Christ our own as well. And sometimes his own people are not so ready to accept that. Real peace means a week by week commitment. Real peace means trying out prayer. Real peace means the ability to change our lives. Real peace is hard if we want to make it hard—but it is as easy as anything if we have the courage to go for it.

Another great Christmas theme is to do with 'a Saviour'— 'Saviour, since thou art born .... ' At midnight, in hundreds of churches on Christmas Eve, thousands of people sing these words. But do we want a Saviour? Or do we *need* a Saviour? I find it especially interesting to preach a Saviour in an enterprise culture like ours, where we are encouraged to be in charge of our own destiny and to build our own successes. We praise enterprise and individualism and have come to accept the virtue of self-reliance. In many respects these are all good values and have contributed to massive changes for the better in our own society and across the world.

But as a Church and as a minister, you have to enter a word of caution as well. We have to advise caution, because someone has to tell men and women that in the end we cannot do everything for ourselves and ultimately we *all* need a Saviour. This is not always the most popular thing to say. It risks sounding like failure. It smacks of weakness. It stands somewhat awkwardly in what can be described as a self-made society filled with self-made people. And it sounds like that because, I suppose, it is somewhat out of step with secular thought. Yet people need to be saved—saved from themselves, saved from errors, saved from death. And you have to wonder if Christmas is the time when people sing about a Saviour, but do not want to *think* about it. Jesus in the manger is Jesus on the cross. Jesus the child of Mary is Jesus who rose from the grave to challenge our profoundest notions of ourselves and our real purpose in being alive. And on Christmas Eve, do men and women want to receive that sort of Christ or not?

To the boy the smudge was a flea. I sometimes wonder what Christmas is to us. But to be sure, when anyone comes at midnight, hotfoot from pantomime or from anywhere else, I shall want to talk of love and peace and of a Saviour. And when I do, I hope I make sense. And I hope that they are happy. For if the Church cannot or does not make its people happy, nothing else will.

Epilogue, or Last Call

ONCE more we were together—Rikki, myself and our wives. Supper was over and it was time for our usual means of common relaxation—a game of bridge. The cards were dealt and the four of us poured over them in silence.

'Now, Alastair,' Rikki suddenly said, 'tell me a bit more about those Amalekites .... '

Obviously he had only a few points in his hand and the mind had jumped once more to that testy question.

'Well now,' I began, gathering my thoughts together ... only to be interrupted by an agitated, excited lady's voice.

'Alastair, sit up, shut up and bid.'

Sorry, Rikki, it will just have to wait until another time. But I wouldn't dare suggest that we make an appointment!

Acknowledgments

THESE various studies would not have happened without the help I have received from a few good friends. First and foremost, I should like to acknowledge all the help and support from my own wife, my best friend, who is always ready to offer the most helpful, most honest and most encouraging advice as a listener to my various sermons or talks. I also acknowledge the great support I have been given in this project by our own best friends, Kate and Rikki Fulton. They have both inspired so much of what I have written and I am sure that they will continue to offer that same support in times to come. (Perhaps one day I shall have the conclusive answer for Rikki when he asks me about the Amalekites!) Finally, thanks are also extended to my secretary, Mrs Sheila Syme, who helped in the drafting and re-drafting, then in the production of the final script of this book. I wish, for her sake, that the office computer had been in place sooner!

Alastair Symington
Bearsden 1993